DIGITAL
TRANSFORMATION

**HOW TECHNOLOGY CAN
TRANSFORM YOUR BUSINESS**

NUNO SOARES

R^ethink

First published in Great Britain in 2020 by
Rethink Press (www.rethinkpress.com)

© Copyright Nuno Soares

Cover image © Shutterstock | Alexander Lysenko | GzP_Design

Contents

Introduction

My wife was five years old when she asked Father Christmas for a microscope. She had been well behaved that year, so on the morning of 25 December there was a big, beautifully wrapped box for her next to the fireplace. Her joy when she opened the box and realised that Father Christmas had given her the microscope was immense. How could a five-year-old girl be so happy to receive a microscope? Today, my wife has a degree in microbiology and works for the largest biotech company in the world, Thermo Fisher Scientific.

I was completely the opposite. When I was in high school and starting Year 10, I had to decide what path to choose. I knew this decision was important for my future, but I was utterly clueless. Since I was a young boy, I had liked cars. I had amassed a huge collection of Matchbox cars and knew all the brands and models. I was also a fan of the F1 Championship and Rally World Championship and dreamed of being a professional racing driver. However, my family weren't rich and you don't learn how to drive a car in high school, so this didn't seem to be an option. I remember feeling overwhelmed by this situation, and not mature enough to make this decision. I genuinely had no clue what I wanted to be or do in my professional life.

I decided to have a chat with my parents and ask their advice. My father said something simple: 'You should choose something related to computers. Computers are going to be the future and they will be part of every industry, so you will have more opportunities and you can decide later what may be of interest to you.'

Like any other kid of my age, I'd had computers since I was eleven or twelve (the famous ZX Spectrum and Atari). Yes, I liked to play my games and I had learnt the fundamentals of BASIC (the computer language), but I had never thought of a career in computers. The next day, I filled in my school form and ticked the box to choose the information technology path. The next three years were my best years at school. I had never enjoyed going to school so much. I was so eager and motivated that I was selected by the Computer Language teacher to help him in class during my last year. At seventeen years old, I was assisting my colleagues and helping them to learn computer languages. When

I finished high school, I was able to write computer programs in the most complex computer languages, like C++ and machine code. Today, here I am with a successful twenty-five-year career in IT.

With this book, I hope that my words and advice will inspire you on your future technology decisions for your business, like my father's words inspired me.

Enjoy reading.

PART ONE

TODAY'S BUSINESS WORLD

1

The Business Landscape

Small companies are the heart and soul of our economy and our society. These companies are also known as small and medium-sized enterprises (SMEs) in Europe and small and medium businesses (SMBs) in the United States (US). The classification is based on headcount, turnover and (in the US) ownership structure, although headcount is the most commonly used factor. There is also a slight difference between Europe and the US in terms of the subgroups. In Europe, SMEs are divided into micro companies (with fewer than 10 employees), small companies (between 10 and 49 employees) and medium-sized companies (between 50 and 250 employees). In the US, SMBs are divided into micro companies (with fewer than 10 employees), small companies (between 10 and 20 employees) and medium-sized companies (between

21 and 499 employees). These companies are mostly privately owned, with some exceptions in the US. In this book, I refer to all these small companies as SMEs.

SMEs represent 99% of all private companies in Europe and in the US. The distribution of the subgroups is also similar in both places. In Europe, micro companies represent 93% of all SMEs, while small companies represent 6% and medium-sized companies represent just 1%. In the US, micro companies represent 69%, while small companies represent 15% and medium-sized companies 16%. If we applied the criteria used in Europe to SMBs in the US, the numbers would be even more alike. On both continents, SMEs are responsible for around 50% of employment and turnover.[1]

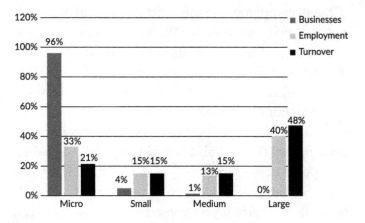

UK businesses by size

1   C Rhodes and M Ward (2018) 'Briefing Paper Number 06152: Business Statistics', House of Commons Library document

In contrast, the remaining 1% of companies, most of which are publicly owned, are responsible for the other 50% of employment and turnover. If we look at these numbers in a pragmatic way, they represent a huge gap between these two groups of companies. Even more shocking is the gap between the SMEs mentioned above: the difference in their profitability is huge.[2] Based on numbers from the UK government in 2019, we know that micro and small companies (99% of all SMEs) have a combined average yearly profit of £8,000, while medium-sized companies boast an average yearly profit of £200,000.[3]

This book isn't about the 1% of wealthy multi-global corporations. They are doing well, and they have all the government help they need to carry on making money, employing people and paying tax. This book is for the 99% of brave SMEs out there, and especially for their business owners. They are the heroes, the innovators, the leaders and the entrepreneurs who are responsible for 50% of our global economy.

Owners of SMEs are not appreciated enough. Everybody wants to be the boss – and in case you're wondering, I'm not talking about Bruce Springsteen. Being the boss is not as glamorous as people might

---

2   C Rhodes and M Ward (2020)
3   Department for Business, Energy and Industrial Strategy (2019) 'Business Population Estimates For The UK And Regions: 2019 statistical release', www.gov.uk/government/publications/business-population-estimates-2019/business-population-estimates-for-the-uk-and-regions-2019-statistical-release-html

think. Many people think of business owners as lucky, but luck is what happens when opportunity meets preparation, as Seneca claimed. Business owners are risk takers; they know that success follows failure and that failure is an opportunity to improve. Business owners are doers, who value progress over perfection. They are the force behind our SMEs and our economy.

This book is for you, the owner of a small company. Small by definition, but large in terms of value. Great for your community, and great for our society. These are the companies that will benefit the most from the **innovation** created by the digital revolution. Innovation is a combination of **power, resources** and **results**. With power, you can have or create better resources. With better resources, you can generate better results. As you will see in the next chapter, innovation is fundamental to success.

2

Scaleups

As a global leader in technology, the UK has been at the forefront of the research, development and innovation that has transformed our analogue environment into a digital one. The world around us has seen giant leaps in medicine, science, agriculture and health, not to mention business and economy. We have been able to take phenomenal strides by embracing technology, but not all companies are created equal. While 5.7 million SMEs are responsible for generating £1.9 trillion for the UK economy, just 36,510 of those companies are responsible for £1.3 trillion of that total.[4]

---

4   ScaleUp Institute (2019) 'ScaleUp Annual Review 2019', www.scaleupinstitute.org.uk/scaleup-review

**5.7 MILLION
SMEs GENERATE
£1.9 TRN FOR
THE UK
ECONOMY**

£1.9TRN

£1.3TRN

36,510 SCALEUPS CONTRIBUTE £1.3TRN OF THIS TOTAL!

Scaleups are the growth champions of SMEs

These companies are known as **scaleups**. The definition varies from country to country and even from institute to institute. I follow the research by the UK's ScaleUp Institute, and their criterion for classifying a company as a scaleup is that it must grow by more than 20% a year by number of employees, turnover or both.[5] In the UK in 2019 these companies included:

- 13,100 registering a growth of more than 20% a year by employing more people

- 30,600 registering a growth of more than 20% a year by increasing their turnover

- 7,400 registering a growth of more than 20% by increasing their employees and turnover

Just 0.6% of the UK's 5.7 million SMEs are accountable for the significant contribution to our economy mentioned above. These companies are not only growing and scaling, but leading the way in business performance, productivity and profitability. They are not

---

5   ScaleUp Institute (2019)

necessarily the big companies that we would associate with significant growth: 63% of these scaleup companies have between ten and fifty employees.[6]

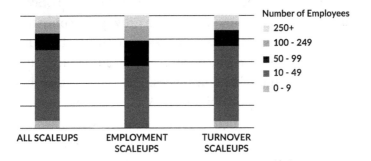

Most scaleups have less than 50 employees, 94% have less than 250.

Why do some companies make the leap to being productive and profitable, but others don't? Many factors affect productivity and growth in an organisation, but one factor influences them all: innovation. Adopting the right technologies in the right areas is the differentiating factor for these scaleups. Streamlining systems, outsourcing to experts and understanding the importance of data and metrics can help a company to grow rapidly, resulting in higher levels of productivity and output. As a global leader in technology, the UK has the ability and the resources available for its SMEs to compete in their respective markets, so why can't we all grow quickly? The problem lies not in the availability of technology but in our ability to adopt, implement and integrate it successfully. We need to

6   ScaleUp Institute (2019)

learn to use technology as a tool to help us do our jobs, develop our strategies and achieve our goals.

I would like to see more SMEs becoming scaleups. Scaling up doesn't mean you have to grow your company to have thousands of employees, a complex structure and a faceless presence. More than half of scaleups have fewer than fifty employees. This is the future; this is where the opportunities are. We need more of *these* companies – not gigantic, ruthless corporations. We need more companies that can create more and better jobs. Companies that provide and promote a modern workplace that their employees enjoy working in. Companies that allow people to build meaningful relationships, internally and externally. Companies with social responsibility for their community. Companies that are wealthy – because wealthy companies can create prosperity, and prosperity will make the world a better place for us all.

3

Opportunities

Our planet is 4.5 billion years old, and we as a species are 2.5 billion years old. We are not the biggest, strongest or scariest animal on Earth, but somehow we have managed to dominate our planet and rise to the top of the food chain. This wasn't always the case. About 66 million years ago, when Earth was still dominated by dinosaurs, something happened that changed things in our favour: an asteroid with a diameter of 10 kilometres smashed into Earth near what today is Mexico. This terrible event caused tsunamis, earthquakes, volcanic eruptions and firestorms across the entire planet. A huge cloud of dust obscured the sun for more than a decade. These events rapidly led to drastic changes in the environment, and the dinosaurs couldn't adapt quickly enough. They became extinct.

Bad for them, but good for us. The extinction of the dinosaurs provided an opportunity for *Homo sapiens* to spread across the globe and reproduce. We became hunter-gatherers, and our brains developed in ways not seen in other species. This was the period that some scholars call the Cognitive Revolution. As we developed cognitive function, we began to make tools, use tactics to hunt bigger and stronger animals than us, and develop a complex form of communication. Around 10,000 BC, the first Agricultural Revolution took place: as we learnt how to domesticate animals and plants, we began to build settlements and start farming. By this time, the human population was between five and eight million. The second Agricultural Revolution took place between the eighth and thirteenth centuries. This revolution was driven by advances in tools and crops all over the world. By the end of the thirteenth century, the world's population had grown to about 360 million. Our survival no longer relied on the food readily available around us; instead, we relied on our ability to produce our food.

A few centuries later, in the 1700s, the Industrial Revolution took place. This went on for about 200 years. At the beginning of the nineteenth century, the global population exceeded 1 billion for the first time.[7] Then, with the invention of the transistor in 1947, we started the Information Revolution, which has now been

---

7   M Roser, H Ritchie and E Ortiz-Ospina (2019) 'World Population Growth', Our World In Data, https://ourworldindata.org/world-population-growth

going on for about seventy years.[8] By the end of 2019, the global population was 7.5 billion.

Can you see the pattern here? As history moves forward, we are multiplying as a species and getting faster at developing new tools and adapting to extreme change. This is pure innovation. Remember, more power creates more resources, and more resources create better results. We have better food, better medicine, better shelter; we have a better life today than we had 25 years ago, 250 years ago or 2.5 billion years ago. It is undeniable: we have always taken opportunities and used them to succeed as a species. This is not going to change.

We can see the same pattern in our companies. In the year 2000 there were 3.5 million SMEs in the UK, and by 2019 there were 5.7 million.[9] This is an increase of almost 40% in less than twenty years. This represents more employment for our people, more taxes for the government and more money for our economy. This can only be a good thing, because it leads to more opportunities for growth that we can benefit from.

As our world continues to transform, so can you and your business. Understanding and overcoming the fears that may be holding you back will enable you to see the opportunities in your industry, not just the ob-

---

8   Computer History Museum (nd) `1947: Invention of the Point-Contact Transister', www.computerhistory.org/siliconengine/invention-of-the-point-contact-transistor
9   C Rhodes and M Ward (2020)

stacles. Working through a digital transformation can be a daunting, exciting and challenging process. Still, with the right advice at your side, you can embrace the future with confidence and clarity, knowing that the decisions and investments you make are based on sound and reliable thinking. When you use technology positively and with purpose, your business can adapt quickly and efficiently while remaining agile in an ever-changing business landscape.

A good example of this is the business opportunity presented by the internet. The internet was born out of the need for the US, the UK and France to share information and knowledge. The development of the Advanced Research Projects Agency Network (ARPANET) in 1969 was the beginning of what we know today as the internet. The World Wide Web was created in 1990, and from the mid-nineties the internet began to revolutionise our culture, commerce and technology. New forms of communication were created, such as email, instant messaging, voice over Internet protocol (VoIP) calls, online video calls, blogs and social media. Platforms were built for shopping online. Although the internet killed many jobs, it created far more. It is estimated that for each job destroyed by the emergence of the internet, 2.6 new jobs were created.[10] This demonstrates that as new technologies

---

10   M Pélissié du Rausas, J Manyika et al (2011) 'Internet Matters: The Net's Sweeping Impact on Growth, Jobs, and Prosperity', McKinsey Global Institute, www.mckinsey.com/industries/technology-media-and-telecommunications/our-insights/internet-matters

emerge, they create the opportunity to do things that were not possible before.

Today, we think of heart transplants and invitro fertilisation as normal. Imagine fifty years ago telling someone with a heart problem, 'Don't worry, we'll remove your heart and give you a new one.' Back then, this was inconceivable, and it was probably considered unethical. Nowadays, we ask ourselves whether we should let our kids access technology from a young age. Controlling their use of technology may seem to be a wise decision today, but whether we will still think that way in the future remains to be seen. What we do know is that progress brings us opportunities. There are always two sides to every coin, but the difference with opportunities is that you can choose which side you want to look at.

4

David Versus Goliath

In 1519, the Spanish conquistador Hernan Cortes landed on the beaches of what is today Veracruz in Mexico. He had eleven ships, six hundred men, fifteen horses and fifteen cannons. In just two years, he had captured the Aztec Empire and subjugated 6 million people. Ten years later, Pizarro Altamirano, another Spanish conquistador, did the same with the Inca Empire, with even fewer resources. In India, 5,000 British officials with 70,000 soldiers and around 100,000 businesspeople and their families ruled over and exploited more than 300 million Indians for 200 years.[11] What the Spanish, the British and the other European colonialists did was unacceptable. What made it possible, though, is that they had better technology: armour, weapons and ships.

---

11   Y N Harari (2015) *Sapiens: A brief History of Humankind*, New York: Penguin

Something similar is happening in the business world.

At the beginning of my career in the 1990s, I got a job in a large global enterprise with more than 1,500 employees and a turnover of millions of euros. This company had the means to invest in and implement expensive technology that most other companies didn't even know existed. I was given the opportunity to work with some small companies that were the partners and distributers of the company I was working for. I was shocked by how differently they operated – the gap between us and them was huge. It wasn't the number of staff or the turnover that stood out to me, but the processes: how slow they were, how complicated and cumbersome their workflows were. It showed me what a difference technology can make. I was living in a futuristic bubble, so when I was confronted with their reality it seemed obvious that they were falling behind and that it would be extremely difficult for them to narrow that gap. These were good small companies, but it was impossible for them to jump on to the technology wagon. Technology was complex and specialised people were needed to implement it, which made the costs too high for small businesses. These companies were the Aztecs, Incas and Indians of their day.

Even today, large companies tend to be more respected and admired than small ones. They have the money to showcase how good they are. Even if we have never used or interacted with them, our perceived image of them is positive. Everybody wants to work for one of the big companies: if you can include them on your CV, their status and prestige are automatically transferred to you. If you work for them, you must be good. This is powerful, and these companies know how to use that power to their advantage. How many times have we seen big corporations challenging governments? These are the colonialists of the business world.

With small companies, it's the opposite. They have to work their socks off to prove themselves. Their circle of influence is also relatively small: if you haven't interacted with them, you've probably never noticed them. Our perceived image of small companies is less positive too, but this is changing. Small companies treat their staff as people, not numbers. They have more impact on their local community, they are more socially responsible, and in general they are more genuine. Technology is helping with this change; as it has become more accessible to small companies, they can take more advantage of new tools than ever before. With their lower costs and easier implementation, these tools are making SMEs more powerful, more flexible and more efficient. By using technology and social media, they can reach bigger and more diverse audiences. They can promote themselves and show the world how great they are, and we can find them more easily too.

I work with a few small companies that have a global presence. These companies have twelve to fifteen employees, are high performers, are flexible and dynamic, have a great culture and take social responsibility seriously. They are competing with the big boys on the same playing field, and they are smashing it. They understand the power of technology and they have embraced digital transformation. They are deeply dependent on technology in their operations, and their staff are tech-savvy team players who genuinely collaborate. This allows them to have simple internal processes that make it possible to deal with things efficiently and produce high-quality work. They know how to use social media in a professional way, positioning themselves so that their perceived image is like that of a large enterprise. Being small is not detrimental; in fact, the opposite is true. Small teams are great performers, easy to manage and flexible. Without bureaucracy slowing them down, they help each other more, are extremely motivated and develop internal talent.

5

Productivity Is Efficiency

Accruing to the *Financial Times*, the UK has a poorer productivity level than that of the other G7 countries, with the exception of Japan.[12] In 1960, we were the most productive country in Europe. Our productivity continued to grow for the next fifty years, but it did so at a slower pace than that of France and Germany, which eventually overtook us. Since the 2008 financial crisis, our productivity has almost stagnated and the gap has been getting wider.

---

12 G Tetlow (2018) 'The UK's corporate productivity challenge, in charts', *Financial Times*, www.ft.com/content/c78ff64c-fc7f-11e7-9bfc-052cbba03425

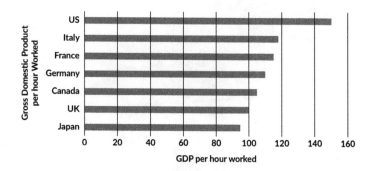

UK productivity compared with G7 countries

Why is this happening? There are a few contributing factors. First, the most productive companies have lost momentum and are failing to improve their productivity. The UK has too many companies with poor productivity levels compared with other countries, and far too few are doing better than average. There is also a big gap between regions in the UK. Outside the south of England there are too many underperformers; Bristol and Reading have a larger share of high-productivity businesses than Sheffield and Hull do. Worst of all, our young workers are low skilled, as found by the Organisation for Economic Cooperation and Development in 2016.[13] Andy Haldane, the Bank of England's chief economist, argued that much of the UK's weak productivity growth can be explained by the large number of 'snails': companies that are often slow to adopt new technology, less sophisticated in

---

13 OECD (2016) Development Co-operation Report 2016, Paris: OECD Publishing, https://doi.org/10.1787/dcr-2016-en

their management practices, less able to raise finance and more domestically focused.[14]

It is obvious that we need to improve productivity and efficiency in our businesses if we want to succeed in the decades to come. But the question is: how?

Better productivity doesn't come from killing yourself trying. Productivity is efficiency. Don't work longer hours; instead, make your working hours count more by focusing your efforts on getting more done in the same period. How many times have you heard someone say, 'Have you seen Joe Bloggs, working twelve hours a day and at the weekends too? He must be doing so well.' But if you mention that you don't work on Friday afternoons, the reaction is usually, 'Oh, that's a luxury; you're so lucky.' It's not luck; it's working smarter, not harder.

How can we work smarter instead of harder? As Andy Haldane from the Bank of England suggests, you should adopt new technologies and bring them into your business. Technology can help you and your team do more with the same or even fewer resources. It can help you optimise your processes and streamline your workflows. Technology is better than humans at doing repetitive tasks, following processes that can be automated, monitoring things, and alerting you or

---

14   D Strauss (2018) 'Is "long tail" of small businesses to blame for poor UK productivity?', *Financial Times*, www.ft.com/content/f5e074ae-9734-11e8-b67b-b8205561c3fe

your team. When you use technology to do the boring stuff (the *functional* work), you and your team can focus on the creative things (the *vital* work). This is where we are better than technology.

If using a piece of technology would save one of your team members four hours a week, as a business owner it is rational to do it. You don't need to sack that person; they can use those extra hours to accomplish other tasks. By saving those four hours you can bring in more business, get more clients and sell more, all with the same resources. Salaries are the biggest bill on your profit and loss report, so if you can increase your turnover without increasing your salaries, that can only be a good thing.

PART TWO

ADAPT TO SURVIVE

6

From Analogue To Digital

'May you live in interesting times' is an English expression that's often claimed to be a translation of a traditional Chinese curse. Our world is certainly changing. Shops on the high street are closing down because we are buying more online. Newspaper sales are falling as we turn to our mobile devices to check the news. The number of pubs has decreased significantly over the last decade, with more of us using social media to interact with family and friends. Many young people have never used a physical map; instead, they use Google Maps for precise directions to their destination. All these examples have something in common: technology. Technology has become an integral part of our lives; it's in our home, our workplace, the supermarket, our car and the palm of our hand. Whether we like it or not, we're rapidly moving from an analogue world to a digital world.

Two main factors are driving this change. The first is the Information Revolution, which started in the 1950s with the invention of the transistor and continued with the proliferation of computers in the 1970s. The second is the transition from the older generations to the younger ones. We'll return to the Information Revolution later; for now, let's look at this generational change. The oldest generation of working age is the baby boomer generation, made up of people born between 1946 and 1964. Then we have Generation X, people born between 1965 and 1976. Millennials were born between 1977 and 1995. Finally, Generation Z includes everyone born after 1996 until the early 2010s.

After the Second World War, living conditions improved and the world economy grew to levels never experienced before. The baby boomers became the biggest generation ever, with around 74 million people. They have shaped society as we know it and pushed consumerism to new heights. They love to own things – houses, cars, appliances, boats, holiday homes, clothes, music – and as the wealthiest generation ever, they have been driving our economy. This generation grew up in an analogue world. The first baby boomers are now over seventy, while the younger ones are over fifty; they have left or are leaving the workforce, and they are either releasing equity by selling their houses or leaving their inheritance to their children.

Millennials are the second-biggest generation, with 71 million people. The older ones are in their late thirties and the youngest are in their early twenties. They share the workforce with Generation X, but they will soon be the dominant generation at work. In contrast to the baby boomers, millennials grew up in this new and different digital world.

Technology entered the baby boomers' world when they were already adults, but millennials were surrounded by technology from the moment they were born. It was part of their development as individuals; they live and breathe technology. In the middle of these two generations we have Generation X, which is probably split in half on the issue of technology. Some will identify more with the baby boomers, while others will identify with the millennials. Generation Z, the youngest, is even more technology-oriented.

Technology is changing how we perceive the world, how we buy or sell products and services, and how we live our lives. It is even changing our spending patterns. Baby boomers love to buy things and are proud of the things they own. On the other hand, millennials rent houses, lease cars and subscribe to music. They are more interested in accessing things than in owning them. This mental shift has repercussions for our companies. Those that understand and adapt to this change will thrive in the decades to come, while those that ignore or deny it will inevitably fail.

7

There Is No Going Back

It's Friday afternoon and you feel the buzz of your smartwatch on your wrist. You give it a quick glance; it's an alert prompting you to move. At the same time, you realise that it's already 5pm. You close your laptop, grab your tablet and put them in your bag. You take your smartphone from the wireless charging dock and put it into your pocket. Outside, you touch your car door handle and the car opens for you. Before you leave, you select Home as your destination on the satnav system. The system tells you that your journey will be delayed by forty-five minutes because of an accident, and asks if you want to change your route. You accept the new route and start driving. Fifteen minutes later, the car alerts you that you don't have enough petrol to reach your destination. It offers to find the nearest petrol station. You select your favourite brand, and your route is recalculated. At the petrol station you pay by tapping your credit card on the pump machine. When you arrive at home, you select 'park assist' and the car parks itself. There are some clouds in the sky and it's getting darker. As you open the door, the lights come on automatically. The sensor in your entrance detects your movement and because it is not bright enough, the lights come on. You take your shoes off, hang up your coat and move into the living room. 'Alexa, I'm home!' All the downstairs lights are on and the sound system has selected your favourite playlist.

Twenty years ago, this might have been the introduction to a science fiction novel. Today, this is reality.

We as a species have developed tools for millennia, from the humble stick to the complex International Space Station. The world is full of tools that we use every day. Most of the time we don't even notice them, but I have serious doubts that we would be able to survive if we didn't have them. Our tools are getting smarter, too. Phones are good, but smartphones are much better; TVs are great, but smart TVs are better. Even electricity meters have become smart. My grandparents would be astonished by the tools we have today, but my daughter doesn't believe that TV was only black and white when I was a kid.

Is this frenetic pursuit of new and better tools ever going to stop? I don't think so. I certainly don't want to give up my 58-inch LED smart TV for a bulky black-and-white one. After you've brushed your teeth with an electric toothbrush, you don't go back to using a manual one. When you first use a smartphone, you can't believe you didn't have one before. There's a lot of useless stuff out there – do you remember the pagers and watches with calculators from the 1980s? For every useless tool, however, we have ten great tools – and we will always need more.

We will never go back. The future is moving forwards, and nothing is going to stop it.

8

Adapt and Change

If change is inevitable, why do some people resist it? Change is often synonymous with fear, and fear signals that danger is near. The Oxford English Dictionary defines fear as 'an unpleasant emotion caused by the threat of danger, pain, or harm'.[15] The human brain is engineered to prioritise keeping us safe. We've barely scratched the surface of the brain's potential, but we do understand the 'fight or flight' response that it triggers in our bodies. Our cave-dwelling ancestors knew that to keep themselves safe, they would need to run or fight. After a time, they also learnt that to ensure their long-term survival, they could evolve: they could learn to adapt and change. They began to build shelters, make tools and wear clothes to keep

---

15 Oxford Dictionaries (nd) 'Fear', https://premium.oxforddictionaries. com/definition/english/fear

themselves and their families safe. As a species, we learnt to protect ourselves by changing. Today, the same instinct to protect ourselves kicks in when we experience other fears, such as losing our job. We still need to adapt and change to avoid becoming obsolete – or worse, extinct.

Our world is changing fast. How we buy and sell products and services is completely different from just a decade ago. We used to buy based on trusted recommendations from our close connections: our family, friends and colleagues. If someone in our trusted inner circle mentioned a product or a service to us, it would influence our decision. Today, we buy based on reviews, and people we have never met have more influence on our buying decisions than our friends. Likewise, outbound sales and marketing (when companies try to sell you their products) doesn't work any more, and inbound sales and marketing (when you want to buy the products) is the new trend. Long gone are the days of salespeople knocking at the door. Nowadays, everybody knows how to avoid the hard sell. People don't like to be sold to, but they still love to buy. Global production and sales are not going down – we produce and sell more stuff every year – but we are changing how we sell and buy, and technology is at the heart of this.

Many business owners struggle with changes in technology because there is so much noise on the subject.

Feeling fear isn't uncommon, and it usually presents itself in one of three ways:

1. Fear of change

2. Fear of the unknown

3. Fear of wasting money

You can go round in circles asking questions. Which software is right for your business? How much will it cost? Can everyone use it efficiently? Do we need regular updates? Can't we just bolt on new bits to the system we are on? What's the competition doing? What method are they using?

If this sounds like you, you're not alone. Discovering which technologies will help you grow your business successfully and deliver a high return on your investment can be a minefield. Don't panic – this book will help you overcome your fears and embrace the technology that's right for you.

9

The Evolution Of Technology

Back in the eighteenth century, the Industrial Revolution was just beginning. During this transition from hand production methods to machines and manufacturing, new machine tools were developed and new chemical and iron production processes were invented. Steam and water were used to power mechanised factory systems. The Industrial Revolution also led to unprecedented population growth. In just two centuries, society went through huge changes. The population had to adapt to new types of jobs, new ways of living and new problems, such as child labour and rapid urbanisation.

In the twenty-first century, we are in the middle of the Information Revolution. Our industrialised society is transforming into a society that is based on information technology. The first working transistor was invented at Bell Labs in 1947. Twelve years later, also at Bell Labs, the metal-oxide-semiconductor field-effect transistor (MOSFET) was invented and went on to become the most manufactured device in the world. This invention of transistors led to the development of computers throughout the 1960s and 1970s. In 1975, a new type of computer – the personal computer, or PC – was introduced to the world. The Altair 8800 was built with the famous Intel 8080 central processing unit. Bill Gates and Paul Allen wrote the BASIC compiler for it and created Micro-soft (yes, the name originally included a hyphen). One year later, in 1976, Steve Jobs and Steve Wozniak from Apple designed the Apple I, and in 1977 the Apple II was launched. These events were pivotal in the digital revolution.[16]

The year 1981 saw another new concept: the laptop computer. The Osborne Computer Corporation introduced the Osborne 1 to the market at a price of $1,795, which is equivalent to $5,352.74 in 2020.[17] The first smartphone was commercialised in 1994, but it wasn't until the early 2000s that this new device became popular – first with the BlackBerry and later with the first generation of iPhones.[18] In 2010, Apple launched the iPad and tablet devices became widely used.

16 Computer History Museum (nd)
17 Centre For Computing History (nd) 'Osbourne 1', www.
    computinghistory.org.uk/det/504/osborne-1/
18 K Jackson (2018) 'A brief history of the smartphone', ScienceNode,
    https://sciencenode.org/feature/How%20did%20smartphones%20
    evolve.php

In 2019, Apple put the iPhone 11 on sale at a cost of around $599, and about 12 million were sold.[19] Fifty years before that, in 1969, NASA launched the Apollo 11 mission and landed on the moon with a crew of three men. Installed on each Apollo command module and on the Apollo Lunar Module was a digital computer, the Apollo Guidance Computer (AGC). The AGC provided computation and electronic interfaces for guidance, navigation and control of the spacecraft. Today, in the pockets of 12 million people we have devices with 7 million times more power than the AGC.

How can this be possible? It can be explained by the exponential phenomenon. Exponential is a mathematical function, and the simplest way to show how it works is to compare it with the 'adding' function:

$$(1+1=2)\ (2+1=3)\ (3+1=4)\ (4+1=5)\ (5+1=\textbf{6})$$

With five iterations of the adding function, the total grows from 1 to 6. Using the exponential function, we will have:

$$(1+1=2)\ (2+2=4)\ (4+4=8)\ (8+8=16)\ (16+16=\textbf{32})$$

With the same number of iterations, the growth is 32 for the exponential function.

---

19 M Jones (2014) 'iphone Timeline: The History of Every Generation in Chronological Order 2007-2020', History Cooperative, https://historycooperative.org/the-history-of-the-iphone

In case you're curious, this also explains why computers work with an octal number system. They have 4GB or 8GB of RAM, and not 5GB or 10GB. The space of a disk is 256GB or 512GB. These are all multiples of 8.

Moore's Law is an observation and projection made by Gordon Moore, a former CEO of Intel, about the increase of power in technology. In 1965 he predicted that every year the production of components in integrated circuits would double. Ten years later, in 1975, he revised his prediction to doubling once every two years. This was accurate until 2015, when the saturation point was reached.[20]

Another interesting concept is the six Ds, which Paul Diamandis explains in his book *Bold*.[21] He believes that anything that becomes digitalised will go through the same exponential growth as computing and will go through six phases: digitisation, deception, disruption, demonetisation, dematerialisation and democratisation.

All the products mentioned in this chapter have gone through these six phases. They apply to new digital products and services as well as old analogue ones that are being digitised. The Internet of Things (IoT) is a great example. Coffee machines can now send you a text message to tell you that they need to be descaled.

---

20 Intel (nd) 'Over 50 Years of Moore's Law', www.intel.co.uk/content/www/uk/en/silicon-innovations/moores-law-technology.html
21 P Diamandis (2015) *Bold: How to go big, create wealth and impact the world*, New York: Simon & Schuster

They know how many coffees you've made since your last order, so they can order more capsules for you automatically.

The evolution of technology is like a fast train – the Shinkansen in Japan or the TGV in Europe. These trains can travel at high speed, but they move slowly when leaving the station. Technology today is pulling away from the station slowly, but soon it will be moving much more quickly so now is the time to hop on to that train. If you and your company don't do it now, it could be too late. Don't stay on the platform, watching these beautiful trains pass by. Be the one sitting inside enjoying the journey. If you want your business to succeed in the next decade, it will be essential to adapt to this new digital world.

10

Business Is Digital

Some businesses have not adapted to our digital world particularly well. Some big – if not huge – companies have failed categorically. Kodak, a camera company, was one of the biggest businesses in the world in the 1970s and 1980s, but it filed for bankruptcy protection on 19 January 2012. Kodak either completely missed or ignored the opportunities created by digital photography. And Blockbuster? Founded in 1985 and expanding globally throughout the 1990s, it filed for bankruptcy protection in 2010 and closed in 2013. Again, it completely ignored the digital transformation and the impact of video streaming. Toys R Us? This huge retail company, founded in 1948 and doing business all over the world, filed for bankruptcy protection on 18 September 2017. It had failed to adapt to online shopping. *Reader's Digest*? I'm sure you remember seeing their magazines and books at your grandparents' house. Founded in 1922, at one point it reached 40 million people in more than seventy countries, via forty-nine editions in twenty-one languages: impressive. The company filed for bankruptcy protection on 24 August 2009 and again on 17 February 2013. It is another example of ignoring the digital transformation.

Unfortunately, there are more examples like these, and more will come. These are big, well-known companies, but there are many more examples of small and medium-sized companies that go unnoticed by the media and are closing their doors because they ignored the digital transformation. It is not possible to have a successful business nowadays without some sort of digitalisation. Ignoring it, or pretending that your business is different and doesn't need it, is reckless. It is no longer a question of *when*, but *how*. If you're thinking, 'Yes, I know I need to invest in technology one of these days,' you're lagging behind. You should be asking, 'How am I going to transform my business into a digital company?' It doesn't matter what type of business you have: even the more traditional ones, like retail, need to be prepared for our digital world. Being digitally prepared is not just about being able to sell products online. That is only one piece of the puzzle, and you might not even need it. A digital business is a business that knows how to operate in a digital manner.

Businesses that understand the power of digital and have adapted to it are thriving. Check out these examples. In 1997, Apple was on the brink of bankruptcy. That year, they brought back Steve Jobs and ten years later they launched the first iPhone. Today, Apple is one of the biggest technology companies in the world with a revenue of $267.7 billion in 2020.[22] It is the master of digital transformation.

Technology is transforming the retail sector too. Starbucks, which was founded in 1971, saw its biggest growth from 2000 to 2008. After the 2008 financial crisis, however, it was struggling. The former CEO Howard Schultz came back and reviewed the company's strategy, with a strong focus on social media.

Everybody seems to love Lego, but ten years ago the Danish company was struggling financially. The management streamlined their operations to focus on digital, creating partnerships with massive hit franchises like *Harry Potter*. Now Lego has its own blockbuster and their toys are so popular that the company is struggling to keep up with demand.

Even technology companies need to adapt. IBM is one of the few companies that managed to stay on the Fortune 500 list for more than half a century. It was the biggest computer hardware seller for decades, yet in

---

22 A Murphy, H Tucker et al (2020) 'Global 2000: The World's Largest Public Companies', *Forbes*, www.forbes.com/ global2000/#5f1855d1335d

1992 it lost $5 billion and almost went out of business. The new CEO, Lou Gerstner, made some changes at great cost, firing almost 100,000 people. He changed the company culture and its marketing strategy, selling the hardware divisions and focusing on business services and software development. The company made $81 billion in revenue in 2015.

No one is immune to this revolution, especially you. The 2020s are going to be ruthless to companies that decide to put their heads in the sand. They will be finished. The only way is digital, and you need to adapt now. In this book, I will guide you through this journey so you can begin your own digital transformation and be one of these successful businesses in the 2020s.

11

Anno 2020

The year 2020 will be remembered for decades. In the face of the COVID-19 pandemic, the world was forced to go digital. Countries all over the world went into lockdown and millions of people were told they had to work from home. All of a sudden, working from home was a must, not just a luxury to be enjoyed by a few. Companies that had invested in remote working before 2020 suffered some sort of disruption, but those that had not really struggled.

Retail companies that had invested in their online presence in recent years suffered too, but not as much as the ones that didn't have an online presence. Companies with digital products, a global presence and a digital mindset went through a difficult period – but they were much better prepared to bounce back and dominate their market.

The year 2020 was bad for our global economy, our local communities and ourselves as individuals, but some good things happened too. Pollution fell to levels that we had not thought possible, rivers all over the world recovered and wildlife populations grew. Some people believe this was Mother Nature's way of warning us to think about how we behave and what we do. Whether this is true or not, the crisis gave us an opportunity to correct our mistakes, to redirect ourselves and to look forward with different eyes. Now is the time to let go of bad habits, preconceptions about certain things, and intolerance towards new ideas and concepts. After a period of reflection, we will have a great opportunity to restart and reset. This is not just a job for states, governments, politicians and world organisations; this is a job for us all. It starts with us as individuals. We must adapt and transform how we do things in our day-to-day life. Our companies need to follow by moving away from the status quo and embracing new challenges.

Working from home used to be seen as less professional than working in an office. Having an online meeting instead of meeting a client in person wasn't seen as being professional enough. Working with people who were based in different parts of the country or the world was seen as being difficult and impractical. Many companies did not allow employees to access social media during working hours. All of this is now called the 'new normal'. We have online meetings at our kitchen table. They are interrupted by our kids or we hear someone's dog barking in the background, and that's fine. Nobody judges these things as unprofessional, because we are all in the same boat. We can look at this crisis not just as a calamity but also as a positive event. It has made us more human, forgiving, understanding and accommodating. We are far less judgemental and more open to different ways of doing things. Above all, 2020 will be remembered as the year when digital transformation changed the world.

PART THREE

GEARING UP FOR THE FUTURE

12

Digital Transformation

What is digital transformation? Buying a load of technology and throwing it at your staff, expecting everything to be different the next day, is certainly *not* digital transformation. The word *transformation* implies adapting to change, rather than starting over and doing something completely different. It's about moving from an analogue to a digital approach.

Look at the example of the car manufacturer Porsche. Porsche is associated with the concept of sports cars – fast, noisy and thrilling. Their petrol engines are positioned at the back, providing a characteristic sound and a unique driving sensation. In 2020, Porsche launched its first electric car. Without the petrol engine at the back, the unique sound and driving sensation changed. It is a completely different product, but it still looks and feels like a Porsche. The manufacturer incorporated digital features into the product while retaining its brand identity. Porsche is still a manufacturing business that produces physical products. Its identity, values and brand are the same. It would have been easy for them to say that it's impossible to create a Porsche without a petrol engine, without that special sound, but they didn't. They transformed, taking the opportunity that embracing digital offered. In almost 100 years, the look of a Porsche hasn't changed much: the silhouette of the 911 has hardly changed since the first model was built in 1964. For a company not used to big change, going electrical must have been a daunting challenge, but they moved out of their comfort zone and boldly secured their future as a market leader.

Watching a live football match on your tablet instead of on your TV is not transformation. Using your tablet may be more convenient, because you can do it while you're on the train or even on holiday, but it doesn't transform the whole experience of watching football. It's the same experience but with a different tool. Transformation should be a whole new approach that breaks the rules and creates new ones. Let me take you back a few years to the time when I used to go on summer holidays with my parents. That was a really exciting time of year for me. I used to share my excitement with my friends by sending them postcards with pictures of the local area. Do you remember those shops with postcard-stands full of beautiful pictures? I used to buy a few, write something on the back, and post them home to make my friends jealous. Nobody does that any more. Why? Because the way we communicate with each other has been transformed. Now we take our own pictures with our smartphones. Better, we take selfies in these special places and post them on social media. The end result is the same, but how we achieve it is completely different.

When IBM created the electric typewriter, that was not digital transformation; it was just evolution. The end result was the same: a piece of paper with words on it. When IBM produced a PC, though, that was digital transformation. You could still print out a piece of paper with words on it, but you could now send an email (words on a computer screen). That transformed how we communicate. This transformation can only be achieved by changing the way we think and how we look at things.

Digital transformation can be frightening and create uncertainty. Making the move to become a digital company won't be easy; great things are not as easy to achieve as small ones. To start your digital transformation journey, you need courage. You need to want to get out of your comfort zone and accept that you need to take risks. Being openminded and curious about experimenting is fundamental. You need to fail to be able to progress, so it's important not to worry about failing. That's how children learn to walk. They fail plenty of times before they stand up and take their first steps.

Your first step should be to develop a digital mindset for you and your company. When you have a digital mindset, you should be able to question everything you have been doing and see it through different eyes. Just because you've been doing whatever you do in the same way for the last ten or twenty years, it doesn't mean that you can't do it differently. What has brought you where you are today might not be able to take you where you want to go in the future.

You need to go deeper to reinvent and reimagine your processes, solutions and products. Let's now take a deeper look at how you can use technology to do this.

13

Technology Is A Tool

Technology is a tool, and just like with other tools, you have specific types of technology for specific jobs. You don't go to your local hardware shop to buy a screwdriver just because it's brand new and all your neighbours are buying it, and then go home and knock down your kitchen wall with it, do you? No, because a screwdriver is not the right tool for knocking down walls. Before you head to your hardware shop, you identify what you are going to do. You might need to knock down a wall or you might need to replace the ceiling light. These are two different jobs, and they need different approaches and specific tools. If you're going to knock down your kitchen wall, you go to the shop and buy a hammer. You go home and release all your negative energy knocking down that kitchen wall. Great – job done! You feel good until your spouse enters the kitchen and sees all the rubble and dust. Now you're in trouble and you have another job to do: clean up all the mess. You pick up the rubble and put it outside. For the dust, you have two options: a broom or the vacuum cleaner. Both will do the job, but one is more efficient. One is also more expensive. That is not a problem, because you know that the vacuum cleaner, the more expensive one, is also more efficient. It will save you time and it will do a better job. I'm not telling you anything that you don't know already, and I'm sure you agree that this makes sense. Tools are designed to help with specific jobs, and some tools are better than others at doing the same job.

Having tools is important, but choosing the right tool for the job is even more important. Knowing how to select the right tool is a skill. Just speak with a professional painter or decorator and they will tell you all about the different brushes available. The difference in the quality of the materials they are made of can change the quality of the painter's work. They use different brushes for different surfaces, and different sizes for different purposes. Painting a living room is different from painting the external walls of a house. Just like a painter understands what type of brush to use for each job, you need to understand what type of technology is right for your company. Painters don't choose a brush just because it's brand new and trending with other painters. The same concept applies to technology: you don't want to invest in technology because it's cool and new; you want to buy the right technology for your company.

To choose the right technological tools for your business, you need to understand how your company operates. In other words, you need to know what your systems are. In the next chapter we'll look at company systems in more detail.

14

Systems

A nything can have a system. The dictionary definition of system is: 'A set of things working together as parts of a mechanism or an interconnecting network; a complex whole.' It is also defined as 'A set of principles or procedures according to which something is done; an organised scheme or method.'[23]

Let's have a look at some examples of systems and the differences between them. In 1913, Henry Ford developed a moving assembly line for the production of a car, the Model T. This assembly line used conveyor belts to move the car from one station to another, dividing the building process into forty-five steps. Using this system, one Model T could be assembled in just

---

23 Oxford Dictionaries (nd) 'System', https://premium. oxforddictionaries.com/definition/english/system

ninety minutes.[24] Ford also implemented a procedure to assign workers to specific locations instead of having them roam around the different sections. This reduced injuries and increased productivity. The assembly line is an example of technology applied to a system. Assigning the workers to specific sections is an example of a system applied to people.

The McDonald's Big Mac is the most famous hamburger in the world. Is it the best hamburger in the world? Probably not. There are plenty of restaurants, pubs and takeaways that sell much better burgers, but a Big Mac is a Big Mac, in any place in the world. If you eat a Big Mac in Paris it will look and taste the same as a Big Mac in Tokyo. McDonald's restaurants are run by young adults; their global average employee age is twenty. How can a bunch of twenty-year-olds be given responsibility for the most famous burger in the world? Because McDonald's invented a fool-proof system to produce the Big Mac: an assembly line for burgers.

Let me share a personal story with you to exemplify another form of system. You've probably noticed by now that I'm a fan of Porsche. Since I was a boy, my dream car has been a Porsche 911 and I haven't owned one yet. Last year, my wife gave me the best birthday present ever: a Porsche Day Experience at their Silver-

24 Ford (nd) '100 Years of The Moving Assembly Line', Ford.com, https://corporate.ford.com/articles/history/100-years-moving-assembly-line.html

stone Centre in the UK. As you can imagine, that day I was a little boy again. Here I am in a beautiful 911 with a professional driver sitting next to me. We did a couple of laps so I could get used to the car. Then my professional driver got me to stop the car so he could ask me a few questions.

'Tell me what goes into your mind when you are doing the corners?'

'I brake hard before I get into the corner, then I use the apex [the red and white stripes painted on the track] to calculate the best trajectory, and then when I feel the car isn't going to spin, I accelerate.'

'OK, that's not bad. Let me teach you something so you don't have to rely on your feel for whether the car is going to spin or not. When you start leaving the corner and you start to unwind the wheel, start accelerating. The more you unwind the wheel, the more you can accelerate. This way, the car will never spin.'

And off we went for a few more laps. My confidence went up and to my delight I started doing faster and faster laps. Why? I'm the same driver, using the same car on the same track, but now I feel in control of the situation because the uncertainty has been removed. This guy had just given me a simple system to apply to my driving skills.

Can you see the connection between systems and technology? Technology is great if it is combined with good systems. Good systems are turbo-boosted by technology, not the other way around. Bad systems are also turbo-boosted by technology, but in a negative way: the technology amplifies the faults of the system, rather than correcting them. This is why technology has a bad reputation with some business owners. They buy and put in place technology with the hope that their systems and their work will improve, only to re-alise that now everything is even worse. Everything is more complicated, tasks take more time to execute, staff don't like to use the technology and the company has spent a fortune.

This is why to identify and create your company systems, you need to understand how your company operates. No one knows this better than you do, but you need to store this knowledge outside your own head to be able to create good systems.

15

The Eight Pillars

A ll companies are different. They are different because they are run by people, and people are all unique. Even companies in the same industry are different. Companies that sell or provide the same product or service are different. However, all companies are also all the same.

Look at car manufacturing, for example. There are around sixty car brands owned by fourteen major companies. They all produce the same product: cars. All these cars have wheels, doors, seats and engines, and they all move you from A to B. The companies that produce the cars are also similar. They have factories, they use robots and workers, they sell their cars and they sell maintenance services for them. These companies also have the same structure. Not because they all produce cars, but because any company in the world will have the same structure – at least at its core. If you've studied business management, you'll know that a business is a business, no matter what product or service that business provides. Any company structure has what I call the eight pillars.

The Eight Pillars

In bigger companies, these pillars may be subdivided into smaller ones. For example, marketing can be subdivided into digital marketing, regional marketing, market development, etc. Sales can be divided into inside sales, online sales, technical sales and so on. Bigger companies organise these pillars into departments. The big departments are managed by directors, and the small departments are managed by managers. This creates the typical pyramid structure with loads of hierarchy. Big companies have a vertical structure.

In SMEs it is different. The separation of the eight pillars may not always be noticeable, because the same person can be responsible for more than one pillar. A common example is that the marketing and sales department is managed by the same person. There is nothing wrong with this, but it means that SMEs have a horizontal structure. The point is that all eight pillars exist in any company, no matter what its size or industry.

This is important for digital transformation because today more than ever, these pillars need to be connected. You shouldn't sell products that you don't have in stock. You shouldn't sell products to a client whose invoices are overdue. You need to manage your staff rota to make sure you can produce your products so your sales team can sell them. You need to know how many leads your marketing is generating to forecast your production, so you can predict how much raw material to buy and when to buy it. It doesn't matter whether you are selling physical or digital products or services; this applies to every company. Yes, with some differences and nuances, because all companies are different.

This is where digital transformation comes in. Information and technology (IT) systems are the glue that connects all eight pillars. These IT systems will allow your different departments to work seamlessly, to be connected and in sync. This is what allows companies to be more efficient and productive.

The Eight Pillars

16

This Is Not The Time For DIY

Entrepreneurs and business owners are doers. They build companies and businesses from nothing. They can learn quickly and implement that learning quickly. They learn about sales, marketing, finances and human resources. They roll up their sleeves and do technical work if needs be. This powerful DIY force is what moves you and your business and you can achieve great things with it, but at the same time it can be dangerous because it can stop you moving forward and achieving better results.

As a business owner, you like to be in control; that's why you quit your job and started your own business. It's your business, you're in charge, and you tell everyone what to do and how to do it. You know how to do everything in your company, and you know how to do it well. If you have to jump on the phones and answer the incoming calls, you will do it as well, if not better, than your receptionist. This is great, because as the owner of your business, you need to understand everything that is related to it. Your staff will respect and admire you because you walk the talk, and they'll feel reassured that the business is in good hands. However, this trait becomes a problem when you get too excited and start to interfere with your staff's work all the time. It's even more danger-ous if the task is something that you enjoy or have some sort of interest in.

Fairly often, I come across business owners who like tech so much that they decide to set up their own IT systems. Playing with tech is exciting for the business owner's mind: they get to learn new stuff, discov-er how things work and then make it happen. This doesn't happen as much with accounting. I'm sure you know your business numbers and you know how to interpret a profit and loss report. I'm also sure that you don't care that much about the process of working the figures out so you have an accountant who does this for you. Whether you know how to do it or not, I doubt you tell your accountant that you're going to process the salaries this month, be-cause you are bored and you want to do something exciting. The words *exciting* and *uninteresting* are the key. If you are uninterested in something, you will find someone else to do it for you. If you are excited about it, it will be more difficult to let it go. This is a big mistake: just because something is exciting, it doesn't mean you should take it on.

I know better than anyone that technology can be exciting and addictive. If you feel the same, you need to treat technology in the same way that you treat the boring accounting (or, if you happen to be an accountant, whatever task you find uninteresting). You need to know how your company technology systems work and what is involved, but someone else needs to be responsible for them. It doesn't matter if this is someone internal or an external IT provider. What's important is that it shouldn't be you.

Let's say that you decided to buy and install a wireless lighting system at home and link it to your Alexa so you can use voice commands to switch your lights on and off. This is quite a fun thing to do, and you want to impress your kids. Unfortunately, you don't manage to install it properly and Alexa starts turning the lights on in your bathroom instead of your kitchen. The motion sensor in the entrance hall turns the lights on in your children's bedroom instead of in the entrance. Nothing serious will happen; you'll probably laugh about it and then go back to using switches. Your partner will not divorce you and your kids will still love you. If you start playing with technology in your company, though, it's a different story. You don't play with your VAT returns, because the consequences could be extremely damaging for your business. Likewise, you shouldn't play with your technology systems. Your business depends on technology to run, so don't mess about with it. Work with a technology expert, be in control, understand what is going on and what is needed. Ask for the advice you need to take the right decisions, but then let the expert do their job.

17

Build A Team You Can Trust

You can't do it all yourself; to successfully transform your business into a digital enterprise, you'll need experts to help you. Bringing in new skill sets, knowledge and expertise will enable your business to grow quickly. You need to choose the right people for the right roles, but you don't need to hire them all and bring them in-house. You can delegate work to external or remote workers; for example, a virtual assistant (VA) for administrative tasks, a marketing specialist for communications, or a specialist HR company for talent management. You can take advantage of all these experts in their field without having to take them on as full-time employees. Consider them as partners in your business, not just suppliers or providers. Let them share your vision and become part of your core team.

One of the reasons UK businesses are falling behind in productivity is that they are throwing people at the problem. This is good because the unemployment in the UK is low compared with other European countries.[25] Expecting that adding manpower to the problem will be the solution is like going back to the 1900s. Even then, Henry Ford didn't hire more workers; he invested in technology. A typical situation that I see in struggling businesses is when the business owner hires a full-time personal assistant (PA) to help with admin and routine tasks. The business owner is right to stop doing these tasks. It's important that they are done to keep the business running, but the owner should be concentrating on things that add more value. However, hiring a full-time PA to help is a big step. A PA won't produce anything that the business can sell, so they are a liability and not an asset. The company's costs will go up without adding anything to its turnover. Delegating this type of work is not easy either. If the business owner has been doing those routine tasks for a long time, figuring out how and what to delegate is going to take time. At first, they probably won't have enough work to keep their PA busy all the time.

This example isn't meant to show you why you shouldn't get a PA. You should get a PA, but instead of hiring someone full time straight away, which will

25 H Plecher (2020) 'Unemployment Rate in Member States of the European Union in January 2020', Statista, www.statista.com/ statistics/268830/unemployment-rate-in-eu-countries

place a heavy burden on your finances, start with a VA. They will do the same job, if not better. You can try different people until you find the right one, without any hidden costs. Hiring someone full time involves huge costs, but when you outsource work to a VA you just pay for the time you use. You can start small and simple, delegating a few things. This will help you to learn the best way to delegate. It is far less scary, because you don't feel that you have to delegate everything at once and you can retain a sense of control. You can do it little by little and when you see the benefits, this will encourage you to keep going.

Crowdsourcing is a great tool for building your team while keeping your costs down. Let's say you need to create a brochure for one of your products. You can plan a draft yourself, then crowdsource a copywriter to write compelling text, and then crowdsource a graphic designer to create the brochure. Better still, you can crowdsource these professionals from a different time zone to get things done more efficiently. If someone is on the other side of the world, you can send them the work when you're finishing your day, they will do it while you are sleeping, and you will have the work done by the time you get into the office the next morning. This mentality will give you flexibility, speed, power and the financial advantage that you will not have if you start hiring full-time people. You should still have a core team that is close to you, but for most business tasks you should crowdsource or outsource them.

Entrepreneurship is not a solo game. You can't grow or scale by yourself; you need to have a team around you. It doesn't matter whether it's a local team or a global one. It doesn't matter if they work full time or part time. They could be sitting next to you in your office or they could be on the other side of the world.

Trust takes time to build. You don't need to physically shake hands with someone and look them straight in the eyes to build trust; you can build it through interaction and reiteration. If you sit next to the same person every day on the Tube but you never interact with them, you won't build trust. On the other hand, you can build trust with someone who you interact with online. Whether the relationship is in person or online, there are some guidelines to follow to avoid disappointments.

Look for people who share the same values as you and create a culture of collaboration and innovation. Align your goals with one another so you are working towards the same outcomes. Creating successful collaborations is all about effective communication and shared values. Do your research and find the right partnerships for your business and theirs to flourish.

18

The Modern Workplace And Workforce

We used to work outside, hunting animals and gathering berries, roots and plants. We were exposed to the elements and we were free to do our work whenever we wanted or needed to. After the Agricultural Revolution, our lives revolved around cultivating crops and raising livestock. We lost the freedom to roam; we started to build settlements and our lives were confined to them. With the Industrial Revolution, factories came along. Our jobs were done inside industrial buildings. We were no longer exposed to the elements, but factories weren't healthy places to be, and the working conditions were poor. Small settlements were transformed into towns and cities housing huge numbers of people. More of us began travelling to work, and natural light wasn't needed for production. This was the beginning of the nine-to-five working day and commuting as we know it. Our factories are now better places to work, and most of us spend our days in comfortable offices.

Where are we going to work in the future? Everywhere: in the office, at home, in coffee shops, on the train and abroad. It doesn't matter where you are any more. The future will bring back our freedom to work whenever and wherever we need to. Working from nine to five (or from eight until four) for five days a week doesn't make sense any more. Having to commute every day for two hours makes even less sense. In our society, this rigid scheduled system is obsolete. Flexibility is key, and it allows us to have a better life. It lets us reclaim our freedom and find a better balance between our work and personal life, making it possible to create a unique lifestyle.

The companies that understand this will be the frontrunners. They will create flexible workplaces that will reduce costs, save time, improve the environment, create social equilibrium and raise levels of happiness. To begin with, premises are a huge cost for any company. Then there are the operating and maintenance costs, including electricity, heating, water, cleaning, insurance, furniture and taxes. Time is the only thing that we can't get back, and we waste a lot of it on commuting and business travel. In 2018, people in the UK commuted for an average of 58 minutes a day.

In London, the average was 79 minutes,[26] while in Tokyo it was a staggering 116 minutes[27] and in New York City it was 72 minutes.[28] All this commuting is expensive for commuters, cities and countries, and we are all aware of the impact on the environment.

Flexible working, if not done properly, risks creating social isolation. Done well, it strikes a much better social balance. Family life improves and parents can raise their kids in better circumstances, spending more time with them and being more supportive. People have more time to build relationships with their neighbours. If you're not convinced, check out the annual *World Happiness Report* published by the United Nations Sustainable Development Solutions Network.[29] In the 2019 report, the top five countries in the world in order of happiness were Sweden, Finland, Norway, Iceland and the Netherlands. Denmark was in seventh place, the UK was fifteenth, the USA was nineteenth and Japan was in a miserable fifty-eighth place. The Nordic countries, which are much more flexible and open, were ranked as the first,

26   TUC (2019) 'Average commuting time is up 21 hours compared to a decade ago finds TUC', www.tuc.org.uk/news/annual-commuting-time-21-hours-compared-decade-ago-finds-tuc

27   RealEstateJapan (2017) 'What is The Average Work Commute Time in Japan?', https://resources.realestate.co.jp/living/average-work-commute-time-japan/#:~:text=The%20majority%20of%20 respondents%20(85.2,in%20the%20NHK%20survey%20above

28   M Kolomatsky (2018) 'Think Your Commute Is Bad?', *New York Times*, www.nytimes.com/2018/02/22/realestate/commuting-best-worst-cities.html#:~:text=New%20York%2C%20with%20an%20 average,by%20the%20typical%20New%20Yorker

29   J Helliwell, R Layard and J D Sachs (2019), World Happiness Report 2019, https://worldhappiness.report/ed/2019/#read

second, third and seventh happiest countries in the world. We should be looking at these examples and learning from them.

It isn't just the workplace that's changing; the workforce is, too. Let's go back to the agricultural age again. In this period (between the eighth and the eighteenth century), people who owned land were rich. Land was a huge asset, and it was used to generate money from agriculture and livestock. This involved intense manual labour, so the landowners needed a lot of people to work on their land. They were called peasants, but I'm going to call them 'cogs' because their jobs were monotonous, repetitive and low skilled. The workers were easily replaced and they were cheap, just like cogs. Large numbers of these jobs were available. Most of the active population worked in the fields, doing physical hard work for long hours in return for peanuts.

Then the Industrial Revolution happened, and the landowners started replacing people with machinery. Machinery is quicker and cheaper, doesn't complain and doesn't get sick. Human cogs were replaced by industrial cogs. This caused a massive layoff and huge numbers of people lost their jobs. Unemployment was something that had never been seen before at those levels. However, this horrible situation was the beginning of a great opportunity to come. Industrialisation and capitalism flourished, and factories started popping up like mushrooms ready to be filled by unemployed human cogs. They were now called the proletariat, but I'm still calling them cogs. Why? Because their jobs were still monotonous, repetitive and low skilled. They were easily replaced, and they were cheap. They were still working for long hours, some still doing hard physical work in not-so-great conditions. The fields had been replaced by factories, and the workforce was doing industrial jobs instead of agricultural ones.

The industrial age (between the eighteenth and twentieth century) saw the industrialisation of all sorts of sectors, such as textiles, mining, chemicals, transport and food. This proliferation led to some great improvements in standards of living, literacy, housing, sanitation, food and nutrition, clothing and consumer goods. The population grew, which created a new opportunity. With a bigger population, more of the new goods being produced in our factories could be sold. The service industries were born, and there was a boom of companies in distribution, retail, sales, marketing, media, real estate, telecommunications, technology and consulting, among others. That meant more jobs for our increasing population, the so-called white-collar workers. Again, I call them cogs. Why? Because their jobs are monotonous, repetitive and low skilled. They are cheap and easily replaced. Today, most of us work in nice comfy offices from nine to five. We don't do manual labour but we process information. While machinery was the cog that replaced manual labour, software and artificial intelligence will be the cogs that replace information-processing work.

Sooner or later, all the cogs working in offices will be replaced by digital cogs. Digital cogs are more efficient, quicker and cheaper. They don't have family, they don't get sick and they don't complain about not having enough breaks. They do repetitive tasks better than humans do. History repeats itself, and the digitalisation of repetitive work will create massive unemployment again. The question is, what new opportunities will arise? Most of them we can't predict, but something I'm certain of is that a cog can't be creative. Creativity is what defines us as a species. It isn't just about art – you don't need to be a painter, a sculptor or a musician to be creative. All the cogs that have replaced the boring work were invented by creative people. If creativity can't be replaced by cogs, the jobs of the future will be jobs where creativity is the main focus.

How do you measure creativity? When you are creating something, time is not important; what's important is the result, the value that is created. Time will still be exchanged for money, but the modern workforce will be measured by the value of their work, not by the time they spend on it. It won't matter if you sit at an office desk from nine to five or if you work from home at irregular and unorthodox hours while you look after the kids. It won't matter if you spend two hours travelling for a business meeting with a potential client or if you have the meeting online at home. What is important is the result, not how you get that result. The new workforce is going to need people with special skill sets, with an amazing ability to learn and adapt to new situations, and with an aptitude for flexibility and creativity. They will not be focused on time; they will be focused on results. Results are what make the world move forward, because results create value.

PART FOUR

YOUR DIGITAL TRANSFORMATION JOURNEY

19

Digital Transformation Strategy

Our new digital world will be exciting, scary, unpredictable and full of opportunities. Let's not fool ourselves; this change is going to happen whether we like it or not. There's no point in denying it: no one is going to stop sending emails and start sending letters again. Business is going to be digital in the future, so we need to adapt to survive.

The good news is that the opportunities are immense. Digital transformation is creating new business opportunities, new products and services, and new jobs. You just need to be open to this transformation, to embrace the change and the challenges that come with it. Choose to feel hopeful instead of scared. You have done the most difficult thing: starting up and running an SME. That's a great place to be. The next step is to transform your company into a high-performance scaleup. Take the lead through innovation and by adopting new technologies to move your company forward. Implement or optimise systems by using the right technologies across the eight pillars in your company. Build your dream team, promote a modern workplace and invest in a modern workforce.

The recipe is not a complicated one; there are plenty of examples of companies that have followed it. It is not a secret either; the resources are out there for you to take and use. What is stopping you is probably a lack of method, a 'how to' guide. Don't worry; my CLEAR method will help you create your digital transformation strategy and implement it success-fully. We'll look at each step in detail over the next five chapters. For now, here is an overview of each step in the method:

- Conscious. In this initial step, you will identify and understand what you have and what you need. You need to know everything about your business: all its workflows, processes and procedures.

- Learn. Now that you know your 'haves' and your 'needs', the second step is to learn and understand what options are available. This is fundamental, because to be able to choose the right options for your business, you need to have a clear understanding of what you could achieve.

- Engineer. From the previous two steps, you will have enough information to start planning and designing the right solutions. It is important that you have more than one option.

- Achieve. This is where you will implement the right solution so that your digital transformation will take shape.

- Resources. Throughout your journey, you should be able to identify any resources you need to successfully implement your digital transformation – from equipment to staff. This step gives you resources that will help you work through all the other steps, so you can dip in and refer to it as you go along.

With a clear plan for your digital strategy, you will have a greater chance of success. Most importantly, you will know how to deal with the unexpected and any difficulties along the way. Let's get started.

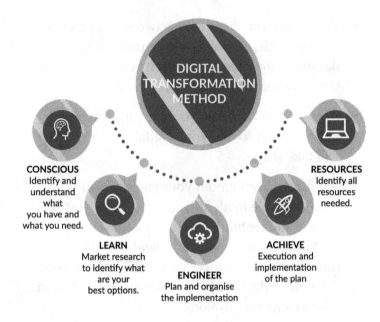

CONSCIOUS
Identify and
understand
what
you have and
what you need.

LEARN
Market research
to identify what
are your
best options.

ENGINEER
Plan and organise
the implementation

ACHIEVE
Execution and
implementation
of the plan

RESOURCES
Identify all
resources
needed.

The Digital Transformation Method

20

Conscious (C)

No one knows your business better than you do. No one is more aware of what you have and what you need for your business than you are. To improve how your business is managed or to make it more efficient, you need to identify and measure everything. You can and should improve everything, not just the things that aren't working or the ones that are causing issues. Just because something is working well enough, it doesn't mean that it can't be improved.

Identify

This initial step is to **identify** what you have and how you do things. You are going to map out your business.

For now, I want you to focus on what you have. We'll think about how to improve it later.

We are going to break down your business into a sequence of **activities**. These activities are your jobs or your processes. Examples include onboarding a new client, invoicing a client, producing a product or processing salaries. These activities should be high level and generic. List all your business activities in an **activities list**. You can download a template to help you with this task at www.digital-transformation.website/resources

Do you remember the eight pillars? The next step is to create a separate activities list for each pillar. You can use my eight pillars or you can adapt them to suit your business. For example, 'Onboarding a new client' goes into your sales pillar, and 'Processing staff salaries' goes into your finance pillar. Take time to do this; don't rush it, because this process is fundamental for the next steps. Work with your team to make sure you have identified all your business activities. You can add more activities later, but aim to identify at least 80% of them before you move on.

After you have created your activities lists, you can break down your activities even more. You can do this by using my **WOP** method: **w**orkflows, **o**perations and **p**rocedures. Let me explain these in detail.

Workflows

My intention here is to help you create a high-level map of your company by visualising your flow of activities. First, you need to identify your processes. To make things easier, use the eight pillars concept and group your processes under each pillar. Visual is the key word here. Don't stress if your drawing skills are not great; this exercise is for your and your team's eyes only. It doesn't need to be perfect. Use whiteboards or a large sheet of paper to draw your workflows. You can take pictures of these drawings with your smartphone and use them later in your documentation. Create one workflow diagram for each activity in your activities lists. This will help you break down your activities into smaller ones. These smaller activities are your **operations**, and they can be divided into two types.

Operations

Each of your operations is either a **task** or a **decision**. The sequence of your operations is what allows you to execute an activity from beginning to end. Your tasks will be represented in boxes, and your decisions will be represented in circles. Use arrows to identify the flow of your tasks and decisions. Let's use the example of the 'Onboarding a new client' activity. We are going to break down this activity into operations and create a **task list** for the activity. This helps you to be more specific and add detail to your activity. In our example, the tasks are represented by the boxes labelled 'Client confirmation', 'Email NDA', 'Create contract document', and so on. An example of a decision is the 'Wait for signature' circle. Two things can happen here. First, the client hasn't signed the contract and you want to remind them. This leads you to the box 'Send reminders every five days'. If after fifteen days you still don't have the contract signed, you want to inform your sales rep and stop the process. The second option is that the contract has been signed, and you want to ask Finances to set up a Direct Debit payment. This task is going to stop your activity and probably initiate another activity under the Finances pillar. To help you complete this exercise for your own business, you can download templates from www.digital-transformation.website/resources. Make sure you identify all the tasks and decisions and their multiple options. Some will be more difficult to identify. Work with your team to make sure all the operations are documented.

Procedures

Workflows and operations will give you a high-level visualisation of your business. Now we want to get into the nitty-gritty of your operations. Your procedures have to be as specific and detailed as possible, because this is where you identify **who** will carry out your operations, **when** they will do it, **what** they will do and **how** they will do it. This is also known as your **standard operating procedure (SOP)**. There are many methods and theories for SOPs, and you can research them online. My version is simple. First, download a procedures document template from www.digital-transformation.website/resources. As you can see, it is a simple document with a table and bullet points. What is important here is to provide as much detail as possible about who does each task, when the task needs to be done, what is done and how it is done. This is important for the next stage, because you can only improve what you can measure.

Measure

Now you have a perfect visualisation of your business, let's add another layer and **measure** your activities. This may be a delicate and sensitive subject for you and your team. Most of the time, people associate measuring with being evaluated. Just think back to your school days, when your grades could make or break your future. Instead, measuring should be about assessing where you are now so you can move to where you want to be. Communicate this clearly to your team. You don't want them to think of you as Big Brother, spying on them. This is to help them and the company to improve and become more efficient. Everybody will benefit. When everyone is on board with this idea, measuring is not a problem.

First, let's measure time. On your procedures documents, take notes on how much time you and your team spend on executing each procedure. Don't guess. Your smartphone has a stopwatch, so use it. Measure each procedure more than once, so you can calculate averages and spot exceptions. Why did a task take fifteen minutes one time you measured it, but three minutes the other ten times you checked? Measure everything for at least a week, ideally from four to six weeks. Not all tasks are done daily, and you will have different cycles: weekly, monthly, quarterly and annual. Include as many tasks and measuring points as possible, but focus more on the frequent tasks then on the infrequent ones. If a task is done ten times a day and you can save two minutes each time, you'll be saving twenty minutes a day, more than seven hours a month and eleven days a year. Tasks with longer cycles might not produce such a big time saving.

Now let's measure iterations. Iterations are things like the number of steps needed to execute an operation, how often an operation is executed, and whether an operation is executed sporadically throughout the week or all at once. Usually, optimising iterations will improve efficiency and productivity as well as saving wasted time. This optimisation minimises errors and risks, and usually improves the quality of the work and the efficiency of the execution.

You can download templates to help you do these exercises and simplify your processes from www.digital-transformation.website/resources

21

Learn (L)

In the previous step, you identified and measured your business. You created a visual picture of your workflows and operations. You then added detail to these workflows with your procedures documents.

The **Learn** step may be the most challenging part of the process. This is where you will tap into areas that you are not familiar with or don't understand fully. This is why the previous step, **Conscious**, is the most important. If you have done that, you will be ahead of many other businesses. Few businesses spend time doing this exercise, and that's why they can't grow and scale in a sustainable way. Having this knowledge about your business will make the decisions that come next much easier, because you won't have to guess or rely on your feelings. When you have the data, you have the information you need to support your decisions about making improvements.

Improve

You can improve your operations in two main ways: **optimising** and **innovating**. Optimising means looking at your existing operations and focusing on time and iterations. Can you save time? Can you reduce the number of iterations? Do you need to train your staff? Do you need to buy equipment that can do the job faster? Optimising is the easiest and the quickest way to make improvements, and you have everything you need to do this. Go back to your procedures documents and look for your measurements. From there, you will have a good understanding of where you can make some optimisations.

Improving by innovation is the more challenging task, because this is where you need to look at your operations with fresh eyes. It's about looking for different ways of executing your operations. Remember the example of Henry Ford and the moving assembly line? By using innovation and not just optimisation, he completely changed how cars were built. You can be innovative by being aware of the technologies available and understanding which are the right ones for your business. Technology is just a tool, but you need to select the right one. Don't try to squeeze a technology into your operations – or even worse, squeeze your operations into some trendy new technology that isn't right for your business. That will only be frustrating and a waste of money. No real improvements or results will come from that approach.

Research

First, you need to research the market and look for technologies and solutions available for your industry or sector. Here are a few guidelines to start with:

- **Google is your best friend.** Google will give you lots of options. Visit the websites that come up in your search, read their blogs, read reviews and watch videos or webinars. There is a ton of information available online, so take your time and access as much as possible.

- **Seek advice from your industry.** I'm sure you know other companies in your industry, or you are member of an industry community. Speak with these other business owners and ask them what they are using and how they are doing it. You'll be surprised by how much people like to share their experiences.

- **Bespoke or not bespoke?** Many business owners believe a bespoke tech system will bring them the growth and profitability that their company needs. As a unique business, you need a unique and special solution... or perhaps not. It's a myth that you can create a system that matches your business needs 100%. It's simply not possible, so why waste your money trying? It's like trying to hit a constantly moving target: you forgot about something important, your needs have changed, the business has moved on, or what was necessary before is no longer a factor today. You need to create an agile and flexible business, and that means your business will be continually evolving and changing, so your system will need to be able to adapt and change too. Spending money on a bespoke system when it will only do a precise job for a particular moment isn't worth the investment.

- **Don't get too excited.** Be cautious about advice from suppliers who sell or implement just one solution. Usually, they don't care about your needs; they just want to sell their solution. They will tell you that their solution does everything and anything, that it's the all-singing, all-dancing solution for you. Maybe that's true, but be cautious and research more options.

- **Trust the experts.** Believe me, we've all made mistakes, and experts are no exception. In fact, they've probably made more errors than anyone else in their search for innovative ideas and concepts. That's why it's good to talk to the specialists when you're choosing the right technology for your business. Understanding which hardware to choose and which software it will talk to can be a minefield. Everything is interlinked and connected these days, but it's easy to miss something or make the wrong connection – and we all know the result of a bad connection in business. You can avoid costly mistakes by using an expert. The right tech specialist will help you understand which technology will help you achieve your goals, get you there faster and avoid a bad investment.

• **Look for impartiality.** Ideally, you should use an expert who is impartial and doesn't have any financial connections with the suppliers. Look for a technology consultancy or consultant. They make money by selling their experience, their advice and their time, not by earning commission from third-party solutions. Experts who are impartial will make your company's interests their priority.

At this stage, be open. Don't discard something because you don't like the look of it or you want some specific feature that isn't available. Most importantly, don't look at pricing and costs. You aren't making any decisions or committing to anything for now; you're just learning about the options available. Look for as many solutions as possible to stimulate your imagination and creativity. Innovation comes with new ways of doing things, and this is a discovery stage. It's not about what you have, but what you want. We don't always know what we want, so be open and explore different approaches. Let yourself dream, and don't put the brakes on. This is the stage when you can go wild without being afraid.

Now an important note. This can be an exciting and addictive exercise, and it's easy to spend hours researching options. Before you start, set a timescale. It could be a number of hours or a specific date to finish by. I like to use a combination of both. Normally, I decide how many hours I need and set a deadline. Logging the time spent on this task is an easy way to control your time and effort. There is a section for this on my **comparison** document, which you can download from www.digital-transformation.website/resources

Compare

All this research is going to generate a lot of information, and you need to look at that information with a pragmatic and impartial eye. It's important to use the same baseline to compare the different technologies and solutions. You need to compare apples with apples. The best way to do this is to create a comparison document, or you can use the one available from www.digital-transformation.website/resources

This is a checklist document that uses the information from the **Conscious** step and the research you have done already. Here are some guidelines to help you compile your comparison document:

- **Document everything.** When you start looking at the various options, start with cloud solutions, software applications, and technology or solutions provider websites. Read their documents, blogs and marketing material. Watch their webinars and videos. Look for videos on YouTube; plenty of people are doing reviews and testing. Keep it there; don't do demos or start trials. Leave that for later. If you go in too deep, you will be in trouble, so control yourself and don't get too excited. Use the comparison document to record all the features and functionalities of each solution so you can compare the options in a more objective way. Take note of every detail, function and feature. Later, this will help you to separate the wheat from the chaff.

- **Don't forget the pricing.** Now is the time to start looking at prices. At this stage, you don't need to go into much detail. Just add the broad price ranges to your comparison document. This is going to be an investment, not a cost. The **Engineer** and **Resources** steps explain how to analyse and compare prices in more detail. Price is what you pay, value is what you get.

Now you have a perfect picture of your business and a pretty good notion of what solutions you could use. Next, you are going to learn how to select the right tools for your business.

22

Engineer (E)

In the **Conscious** step, you identified and measured your WOPs. In the **Learn** step, you looked at how you can improve your WOPs by optimising or innovating. You also started researching and comparing new solutions. In this third step, you are going to **engineer** your strategy. You are going to decide which solutions are right for your company.

Select

In the **Learn** step, I told you not to put the brakes on and not to discard any possibility. I encouraged you to use the right side of your brain, which controls creativity, imagination, intuition and insight. Now you're going to use the left side of your brain, which controls your analytical thoughts, logic, reasoning and number skills. We are going to bring out the engineer in you. If you're already an engineer, this is going to be easy-peasy.

Let's look at your comparison document. It should contain plenty of options and solutions. If you feel overwhelmed and you're not sure what to do next, that's fine. Before you decide, we need to narrow down your options to between three and five solutions. Three is best, but in specific cases it's OK to go over. At this moment, you know what you have (from the **Conscious** step) and you know what you want or need (the **Learn** step). We need to combine these two, and this is where the **requirements** document is handy. You can download a template from www. digital-transformation.website/resources

Fill in the requirements document with specifications from your WOPs and your comparison document. The requirements document contains a matrix to help you match the solutions you have researched with your requirements. With this document you should be able to objectively select the three solutions that tick the most of your requirements. Don't be surprised if none of the solutions match all of your needs. Usually, a solution that matches 75% to 85% of your requirements is a good match. These three options are what you are going to focus on next.

Now that you have the three best candidates, you can go back to 'research and compare' mode. Now is the time to do the demos and start trials. Do this for one solution at a time; don't start all three at once. You'll probably have a short period of time to try out a solution: usually seven to fifteen days, or sometimes thirty days. The sales team will chase you like dogs, putting pressure on you to make a decision. Take your time: don't let them pressure you and rush your decision-making process. You need to stay in control to get as much information as possible about their solution. Start a new research comparison document for these three solutions. Copy your research from the previous document and add to it as you work through the demos and trials. This is the time to dive deep and look at every detail.

Pricing is your next priority. Make sure you understand all the related costs. Most of the time there are hidden costs, and you should be aware of them. Look for the following things:

- **Length of the contract.** Is it monthly, quarterly, annual or longer? Be careful with long contracts; I'm not a big fan of them. Technology evolves quickly and price changes are usual. Having long contracts can leave you with an obsolete or an expensive solution.

- **Training.** You will need to train your staff. When employees don't know how to make full use of their systems, this leads to inefficiencies and lower productivity.

- **Implementation.** Changing systems or implementing new ones doesn't happen quickly. It can take days, weeks or even months, depending on the size and complexity of the project. Make sure you cover all aspects, including your company down time. Can it be done in phases or in just one weekend? What are the differences in cost?

- **Payment structure.** Do you have to buy the whole solution up front, or can you pay in monthly instalments? Is the cost fixed or flexible? Is the cost per user or for the whole company?

As Warren Buffett said, 'Price is what you pay, value is what you get.'[30] You need to understand the full pricing of a solution, but it is the value that is important. At first glance, £10,000 may seem a lot of money to spend, but if your investment allows you to generate £100,000 then £10,000 is a bargain.

Present

This is the critical phase for your decision. By now, you should have a pretty good picture in front of you, but don't sit in your office alone and choose one option yourself. Good decisions are made by listening to others and collecting as much information as possible. If you have followed the previous steps, you should

30 2008 letter to Berkshire Hathaway shareholders, www.berkshirehathaway.com/letters/2008ltr.pdf

have all the information you need. Now it's time to listen to others. The best way to get honest feedback is to give a presentation. Invite your team and, if possible, someone external to the company, such as a close friend, business coach or mentor.

Prepare for the meeting as if you were going to give a sales presentation. Book your meeting room for half a day, put out some light snacks and present the three best solutions you have selected. Take copies of your research comparison document and give one to each person in the meeting. Bring all the documents you have created so far.

Start by letting everyone go through your documents. Briefly explain each one and then give people time to digest everything. Next, give your presentation. Pretend you are pitching each solution to your attendees. At the end, ask for honest and frank opinions, comments or suggestions. The people in your meeting may bring a different perspective or mention something that you hadn't thought about. This approach will also help you to get some distance from the solutions. You have been working on this closely, testing and selecting each option. This presentation will force you to be objective. You shouldn't think of any one solution as your 'baby'. It has to be the right solution or technology for your company, not for your ego. Have someone else in the meeting take notes for you. The comments and suggestions noted down will be precious when you enter the decision-making phase.

Decide

Now you are going to decide which of your three solutions is the best one for your company. I'm not going to tell you how to do this. We all have different methods of making decisions. Some of us are more logical, while others pay more attention to their gut feeling. Some like to take time to digest it all, while others prefer to make a decision quickly. There is no magic formula here. As Mary Schmich said, 'Whatever you do, don't congratulate yourself too much, or berate yourself either. Your choices are half chance. So are everybody else's.'[31]

---

31 M Schmich (1999) *Wear Sunscreen: A primer for real life*, London: Ebury Press

23
Achieve (A)

You know what is best for your company, but as a business owner you shouldn't be doing everything. Your job is to create and define a strategy, to point and show the way. You should definitely not be executing the strategy; there are people out there who are more suitable for doing that. A football manager doesn't play as goalkeeper, midfielder or striker while managing the team at the same time, so why should you? Like a football manager, you have designed the strategy. You have defined where the team is going and how to get there. Now it's time to hand over the planning and execution of your strategy to someone else. This doesn't mean handing over control. When a football match starts, the manager stays on the sideline, analysing and giving directions to make sure the team is executing the plan according to the strategy.

This is no different. You are the stakeholder and you will be in control.

Outsource

Most of us don't have the internal resources to plan and execute a digital transformation strategy like this. If you do have internal resources, this is a golden opportunity for them to show their value. If you don't, outsourcing is the answer. To outsource with confidence, use these criteria to find the right technology partner for you.

- **Performance.** Look for a company with a record of consistently good performance indicators, not just a company that has done something once. Consider time and volume. If a company has been doing something successfully for ten years, it's not just down to good luck. On the other hand, because some technologies are so recent, time may not always be a good indicator. Another indicator that may be relevant is volume: how many solutions have they implemented? Consider this as well.

- **Respect.** Great companies are respected by their competitors. Ask around and speak with other business owners about them. Has anyone heard of them, and if so, what are they saying? Use your local Chambers of Commerce or other business associations to enquire about them.

These organisations are usually good for cross-referencing opinions and perceptions.

- **Reviews.** These are a popular way of checking up on companies and products. The internet is full of websites and services that publish reviews, so check online. Clients who are either happy or unhappy are more likely to leave reviews.

- **Credentials.** Certifications are important, because they give you an instant indication that a company has a certain competence in a particular field. Be cautious, though, because certifications usually indicate a minimum level of competence. Collecting credentials doesn't make a company an expert.

- **Online presence.** We live in a digital world and the companies you're researching are in the sphere of digital technology. If they don't have a strong online presence, that should raise an eyebrow. Check the company's online presence, starting with their website. Do they have social media accounts on Facebook, LinkedIn or YouTube? Do they have blogs, vlogs, social media posts and endorsements, for example? Research them exhaustively; spend time reading their articles or social media posts. Watch their videos. This will give you a good indication of whether they are the right partner for you.

- **Honesty.** Have meetings and interviews with a company while you are assessing them. One question I like to ask is: 'Give me an example of something that went wrong. What happened and how did you deal with it?' If the provider is honest, they will give you an example. An honest provider will take that opportunity to show you how they managed a bad situation and how they have overcome difficulties.

- **Helpful.** Great companies like to help by solving problems. They'll usually give you something for free or for a small fee. This is not just a sales technique. Genuine companies like to show that they care about you and your problem. They want to connect with you for the right reasons. They are the opposite of companies that want to charge you for everything, even for sending you a quote. Those companies are only interested in themselves and they don't care about you.

Plan

Planning a technology solution project like this is complex and technical. It can take years of experience to do it right, so you need to be able to trust your technology partner and let them prepare your plan. These companies are all different, and there are many styles and methods for planning and executing technology solutions. Different solutions or technologies will require different approaches and have specific needs. However, a few things are common to every project. These are crucial, and a good technology partner should always provide them to you.

- **Overview.** The provider should give you a non-technical overview of the project. This can be done in a Word document or in a PowerPoint presentation, with plenty of graphics to make it easy for anyone to understand the project.

- **Scope.** A project scope document is fundamental for the provider and for you. This is where all details of the project are mentioned. It makes everyone involved accountable: if a task is there, it must be done; if it is not there, it is not in the project scope. This will work for both sides. You will be protected if something isn't executed as agreed, and the provider will be protected if you decide to add something that you hadn't discussed before.

- **Risk assessment.** Any project comes with risks. Risks are not a problem; the problem is ignoring them or pretending they will not happen. All risks should be identified and assessed. What are the consequences? What mitigation actions need to be taken if the risk happens? Which stakeholders will action them? How severe are the risks? Don't ignore risk assessment. Dealing with risks that you're aware of is just part of the process, but dealing with unknown risks can be critical and damaging.

- **Timeline.** This is usually a Gantt chart or something similar. Having a visual layout of the project execution helps to make it clear.

Your role is not to execute the plan but to make sure everything is covered. Make sure everyone involved in the project knows their role and their responsibilities. Be the football manager on the sideline.

Execute

This is the stage when you hand things over to your technical team. You have already done your part, and your technical team will be executing your plan to implement your strategy. This may sound scary and uncomfortable, but believe me, if you have selected the right technology partner, they will do a great job. This is the type of project these companies thrive on. They love doing these things. They have the experience, the knowhow and the right resources to execute these complex projects. Sit back, relax and let them do what they do best.

24

Resources (R)

This step is for you to refer to throughout the process. It gives you more information about what to consider and helps you identify the resources to include or use on your journey to digital transformation. You don't need to use them all; pick and choose the ones that are suitable for your goals.

Documents

The following supporting documents will help you record your journey while using the CLEAR method. You can download them for free from my website: www.digital-transformation.website/resources

- **CLEAR method infosheet.** This gives you a visual explanation of the CLEAR method.

- **Eight pillars infosheet.** This is a visual explanation of how companies are structured.

- **Activities list.** This helps you to capture your activities for each of the eight pillars.

- **Workflow diagrams.** These help you to identify your workflows and create a visual representation of them.

- **Task list.** This helps you to detail your activities. Use it in conjunction with the activities list and workflow diagrams.

- **Procedures document.** This helps you to document your standard operating procedures in detail.

- **Comparison document.** Doing research can be daunting. This document helps you to keep track of it and keeps you focused.

- **Requirements document.** Making decisions isn't easy. This document will help you compile supporting information in a clear format to make the process simpler.

Continuity

Implementing the right technological solution will give your company a great advantage. However, technology is constantly evolving, so it is unrealistic to believe that you will implement a new solution and that will be it. You will need to maintain and update the solution to keep it functional. This continuity is as important as, if not more important than, implementation. Adopting a new technology and then leaving it for years without maintaining it will cost you greatly and put you back at square one. It's like buying a brand new car and never having it serviced. When you maintain your car regularly, it lasts longer and runs smoother.

Most SMEs don't have internal IT resources, because they're too expensive and they quickly become obsolete. All businesses should have a professional information technology managed services provider (IT MSP). Here is some advice on how to select a good supplier.

Size does matter

Don't go for the one-man-band of the IT world. They're the ones who give the IT industry a bad reputation. They can't be in multiple places at the same time, and they can't deal with sickness and holiday periods. Their response times are awful because they are doing everything themselves. Lone wolves are not good in IT, so stay away from them.

Look for IT providers with at least three permanent technicians. This is the minimum that an IT support team needs to be able to cover sickness and holidays and provide services to a decent number of clients. Three technicians will also have enough different skill sets to cover most of the technical issues you experience. A team of three technicians will normally be able to handle around 500 users ('users' means your employees). A team of three technicians should be able to support twenty-five clients with twenty employees each.

Large IT MSPs can also be a problem. When IT MSPs have hundreds of technicians, they tend to organise their technicians in layers. For example, they will have first-line, second-line and third-line technicians. The first-line technicians will be at a junior level and they will be responsible for the initial contact. They'll do the initial troubleshooting and if it's something simple, they may be able to sort it out immediately. If not, they will escalate the problem to the second-line technicians, and so on. This will translate into bad customer service with long waiting periods and backward and forward communication, leaving your staff feeling frustrated and unhappy. Some of the large telecommunications companies are good examples of this type of layering effect, with customers being unhappy with the support they have received.

Look for an IT MSP whose internal structure is based on teams instead of layers. This type of structure will promote teamwork, while removing hierarchy and bureaucracy. Normally, certain teams are assigned to a pool of clients. They will know all their customers' names; they will build relationships with them. They will know the ins and outs of their clients' systems without having to escalate issues to someone else. You will have a better customer experience, and the technicians will feel like part of your company and act like colleagues.

Location isn't important

It doesn't matter if your IT MSP is just round the corner or on the other side of the world. In my experience, 95% of their work can be done remotely, leaving just 5% to be done with an on-site visit or using couriers. A modern professional IT MSP will have secure remote tools. They will be able to monitor your systems and fix them remotely before you've even noticed a problem. Sending someone to visit you every month to do computer clean-ups and check servers is not best practice any more. You don't need to rely on face-to-face interaction to communicate efficiently with your IT MSP. These companies have great collaboration systems for their staff and their customers. Don't discard an IT MSP just because it isn't local to you.

Price versus value

Make sure the IT MSP offers good value. The cheapest providers will fail you. They will overpromise and underperform. They have the cheapest technicians, and they don't invest in training or in the right tools to provide you with a great service. They don't invest in internal processes that result in good customer service. Those companies won't care about you, because you aren't paying them enough. You will just be another client, just a number for them.

To make sure you get good value, ask to see the company's performance indicators. A great IT MSP will be proud to make you aware of them. Here are a few performance indicators that you should expect to see:

- **Percentage of satisfied customers.** I expect the average satisfaction level for companies in the IT industry to be at least 90%.

- **Average first-time reply.** This will give you an idea of how quickly the company will get back to you when you ask for help. The average time in the IT industry is twenty hours.

- **Percentage of reopened tickets.** This will give you an indication of the quality of the company's work. A high percentage of reopened tickets means that they aren't solving their clients' issues properly the first time or that they are rushing to close tickets. This leads to unsatisfied customers and a loss of productivity for their clients.

- **Percentage of one-touch tickets.** This shows you how efficient the company is. When a provider solves issues with just one interaction, it shows that they know their stuff. Bear in mind that resolving more complex issues takes more time and more people, so don't expect to see high percentages here. Anything close to 50% is good.

Budget

The best way to stick to your budget is to set one. A budget doesn't prevent you from spending money; it helps you understand where and when you should invest it. You spend money on tea and coffee, but you invest in technology. The tea and coffee you buy for your office doesn't make you money. It is a cost. It goes into the liabilities category on your profit and loss report. Liabilities take money out of your pocket, while assets put money into your pocket. Technology is an asset; it makes you money. When you start looking at technology as an investment, you understand the need to have a budget for it.

Here are a few points to consider when setting a budget for technology. You should divide your budget into two main sections: fixed costs and variable costs.

Fixed costs

- **Quality.** Devices are not all the same, and it's normal to have a business line and a consumer line. A laptop from a consumer line will not perform as well as a laptop with the same specs from a business line. It will not be the same price,

either; a business laptop will be more expensive.
This isn't because the manufacturers want to
take advantage and charge companies more.
It's because business laptops are designed and
produced with business needs in mind. Business
laptops are designed to be left switched on for ten
to twelve hours a day, while consumer laptops
are designed to be left on for two to four hours
a day. Therefore, the quality of the components
in business computers is higher than those in
consumer computers. On paper, business and
consumer laptops may seem to be the same except
for the prices. You may be tempted to choose the
cheaper one, but in the long run it will be more
expensive, because it will have a shorter lifespan.
Always invest in business equipment.

- **Warranties.** By law, all manufacturers have to
  include a one- or two-year warranty with their
  devices. Business devices must come with a one-
  year warranty, while consumer devices come with
  a two-year warranty. For all business devices, you
  have the option of extending the warranty at the
  time of purchase. Always extend the warranty for
  your devices if you can. It is wise to extend it to
  five years for a server or for a high-end computer
  used for computer-assisted design. For a desktop
  or laptop computer, three years is the minimum
  recommendation.

- **Lifetime.** Different types of devices have different
  longevity. A router or a switch can work perfectly

for ten years, but you can't expect a laptop to work perfectly for more than three years. A server will work perfectly for five years. It's important to know the life expectancy of your devices so you can plan for replacements.

- **Replacements.** Devices will not last forever, and you should have a plan for replacing them. Most of us replace our phones every two years, but the average replacement time for a business computer is six years. A two-year-old phone feels as if I have it for ages; a six-year-old laptop feels like a recent purchase. Having a replacement plan is important for your budget. A simple Excel spreadsheet with a list of all your devices, their purchase dates and the warranty extension periods will be enough. You can download a template here: www.digital-transformation.website/resources

Variable costs

- **Contract length.** Most contracts today are monthly or yearly, but there are still some three- to five-year contracts out there. Run away from those as quickly as possible. Technology moves too fast for you to be tied into lengthy contracts. Whether a monthly or annual contract is better will depend on the context. Sometimes paying annually is cheaper: you may save the equivalent of one or two months' costs. Consider whether it is better for the cost to be an operating expense (OPEX) or a capital expense (CAPEX). You are the best judge of your business's financial needs.

- **Licences.** You will usually need to buy licences for your software and cloud solutions, such as the Office suite, antivirus software, backups, online storage, email systems, accounting software, customer relationship management systems, productivity solutions and collaboration tools. These are usually based on the number of users or devices.

- **Infrastructure.** This includes your internet connections, phone systems, online meetings solutions, remote working infrastructure, IT support contracts, software maintenance contracts, disaster recovery solution, cyber security, IT training and so on.

- **Web.** These costs can fall into your technology budget or your marketing budget. Again, all companies are different. They include your website domain, website hosting and maintenance service, online store, online payment systems and so on.

Variable costs are more difficult to budget for. You will have small and large costs, and they will be charged at different intervals. I like to budget for these as follows. First, create one list of all your monthly costs and another list of all your annual costs. For the monthly costs, calculate how much the annual cost will be by multiplying the monthly cost by twelve. Then add up all your annual costs to calculate your total annual cost. To make it simple, divide that amount by your total number of staff. Then divide it by twelve for a monthly cost per employee. For me, this amount makes more sense and is more realistic to manage. If your number of staff goes up or down, you can easily adjust your budget.

Having a technology budget puts you in control and avoids unwanted surprises. You will always have some unexpected costs, but that's part of running a business. The aim of having a budget is not to set your costs in stone but to plan how, when and where to invest your money.

PART FIVE

WHAT NEXT?

25

The Future Is Here

Over the last twenty years we have seen an explosion in digital technologies. Our world has been transformed from analogue to digital, and what was once science fiction is now part of everyday life. These changes aren't going to stop here, and more digital technologies and solutions will be created and will disrupt our world. In the 1970s and 1980s, many people predicted that by 2020 humans would have been to Mars or even started to colonise the planet – but no one predicted the internet or the transformation it created. If you watch sci-fi films from the 1980s, all the spaceships have cathode ray tube monitors. No one predicted flatscreens or 3D holographic displays. This goes to show how difficult it is to accurately predict what the future will bring, and I'm not going to pretend I can do that. Nevertheless, there are a few emerging technologies and trends that we should pay attention to. Here are some of my favourites.

Telecommunications

The speed and coverage of telecommunications will keep increasing, especially without the need for cables. Worldwide satellite internet coverage will be available by as soon as 2025. Interplanetary internet, which is the ability to take the internet into space, is already being researched. Soon we will be able to access the internet from anywhere in the world. No more excuses for not checking your emails when you're in a remote place.

Internet of things

More and more devices will be connected to the internet. Microwaves, ovens, fridges, washing machines, coffee machines, slow cookers, toothbrushes, shavers, hairdryers, cars and any other device you can imagine will have an internet connection. This is going to completely change how we use and interact with these devices. They will become smarter and easier to use. Your fridge will know what's inside and which products are close to their expiry date. It will be clever enough to order your weekly shop from your favourite online supermarket.

Cloud

The cloud has already entered the mature stage. Anyone with a smartphone is already connected to the cloud in some way. However, when combined with 'internet anywhere' and IoT devices, the cloud will open up endless possibilities. It will facilitate access to huge amounts of data from any device in any location. The cloud will be like a humongous library that anyone and anything has access to. Some research projects are already looking into the possibility of connecting human brains to the internet. Imagine your brain having access to Wikipedia without the need for a device!

Big data

Data is the new gold. The more you have, the richer you will be. Collecting data from different sources and combining it will generate valuable insights. Look at the F1 teams. How many sensors does an F1 car have? How much data is collected from each lap? All this data, collected from different parts of the car, is combined and analysed, giving the F1 teams precise information about the car. Based on that information, the team managers can plan their strategy and make decisions on when to change the tyres or refuel the car. More accurate sensors that can measure a variety of conditions, combined with massive amounts of storage and more process power, will provide valuable insights to companies.

Artificial intelligence (AI)

If you combine big data with AI, you get huge amounts of power. Computer programmers create software to tell a computer how to do things. That means that the results are the consequences of human decisions and actions. Software doesn't forget things or make mistakes, but if the computer programmers have programmed something incorrectly, the software cannot avoid or correct the mistake. AI brings a new perspective, because it can learn from its actions. For example, an AI chess software is only programmed with the basics of chess. It knows the rules and how the different pieces can move. If that software only plays against me, it won't learn how to defeat a chess grandmaster. But if that software just plays against Gary Kasparov, it will eventually be able to beat any grandmaster. AI is going to disrupt us and create a lot of controversy. It will bring good things and not-so-good things, for sure. In the near future, AI is going to force humanity to rethink ethics and society.

Money

Notes and coins will become rare in the near future. Digital money is growing in popularity. We all have debit and credit cards, and we are using them more often to make payments. Our smartphones have digital wallet services, such as Apple Pay and Google Pay. In London, you can use the Tube and pay with your phone. Most retail shops have payment terminals that accept digital payments. Online payment systems like Stripe and GoCardless are also changing how we pay online. Even transferring money to other countries is easy when we use services such as Transfer-Wise. Some countries are moving quickly towards a cashless society. Sweden is leading the way: 80% of Swedes use cards to pay for purchases and four in five transactions are made electronically. In 2019, more than 4,000 Swedes had microchips implanted in their hands so they could make digital payments.[32] Sweden is also considering creating its own digital currency, the e-krona. Cryptocurrency and Blockchain will be the foundations for this shift. Digital money is largely unregulated, and governments will have to intervene to create some sort of order to make it credible.

Automation

Automation has been used and implemented in the industrial sector in particular in recent decades. The car industry is probably the best-known example. Car factories are full of robots and rely heavily on automation. The number of workers in modern car factories is much lower than in the days of Henry Ford's assembly lines. Automation is not just about robots; it includes software, computer bots and AI. Industry sectors

---

32 M Savage (2018) 'Thousands of Swedes are Inserting Microchips Under Their Skin', NPR, https://www.npr.org/2018/10/22/658808705/thousands-of-swedes-are-inserting-microchips-under-their-skin?t=1597332932902

including distribution, agriculture and services will all implement some sort of automation, because any process that is a loop, a cycle or a repetitive task can be done faster and better by technology. Many jobs will be replaced by automation, from robots to software. Agriculture is entering its fourth revolution. The use of AI, the analysis of big data, and developments in drone technology, sensors, machine learning and robotics are changing how farmers are producing crops. Over the next decade, the services industry is where we will see more automation being implemented.

Working from everywhere

Before the COVID-19 crisis in 2020, some companies were beginning to offer remote working to some employees. Working remotely was seen as a perk or a bonus for the privileged few. During the crisis, in just a few weeks the self-isolation measures imposed by countries and their governments forced millions of people to work from home. The technologies that made this possible had been available for years, but companies had been reluctant to implement them on a larger scale. The pandemic simply forced this to happen – and fast. The world has now experienced this new way of working, and companies and workers have realised the benefits. Time saved on commuting and business travel, increased productivity and a better work-life balance have made us question a few things and our perception of remote working has changed forever. Many companies are now pondering whether they need to pay expensive rent and business rates, and whether their expensive travel costs are really necessary. Do they need to pay overtime, or should they just implement flexible working? In the next decade, where we work from will not be important. We will be able to work from everywhere and anywhere.

Social media

Social media is part of our lives, and it isn't just a young person's thing any more. In 2019, Facebook had 2.5 billion active monthly users; in the same year, LinkedIn had 660 million, with 15% being senior-level decision makers.[33] Companies that take social media seriously will grow their business to levels that they never imagined possible. Face-to-face interaction and word of mouth are limited by geography and time. Social media removes these barriers. Companies can research wider audiences at any time, anywhere in the world. Even when you are sleeping, your company can be creating business. Just like print, radio or television, social media is another platform on which you can promote and sell your business. This is changing how companies promote their products and services,

---

33 J Clement (2020) 'Number of Monthly Active Facebook Users Worldwide as of 2nd Quarter 2020', Statista, www.statista.com/statistics/264810/number-of-monthly-active-facebook-users-worldwide; LinkedIn Pressroom statistics, https://news.linkedin.com/about-us#1

and it will continue to do so. Mastering digital marketing and digital media creation will be pivotal.

Space

At first, space exploration was dominated by countries. In the future, companies will expand and finish what those countries started. From the 1960s until the 1980s, the US and the Soviet Union (now Russia) were racing to dominate space exploration. With the dismantling of the Soviet Union, the race ended and countries began to collaborate. A good example is the International Space Station, a multinational project involving five space agencies: NASA (US), Roscosmos (Russia), JAXA (Japan), ESA (Europe) and CSA (Canada). More recently, private corporations like Virgin Galactic (founded by Sir Richard Branson) and SpaceX (founded by Elon Musk) have entered the scene. They will be the new Portuguese and Spanish *Descubridores*, explorers who adventured into unknown oceans in their small and fragile *caravels* to discover new lands and opportunities.

These are just a few areas where technology will have a big impact. To mention them all, I would need to write another book. More important than knowing which areas are going to be affected or relevant is being aware that technology will never stop evolving. Be prepared to keep up with these innovations if you want to be the front runner.

Few small businesses will be involved in developing any of these technologies, but they will have the opportunity to leverage them. Small businesses need to focus on adopting technologies, rather than developing them. SMEs won't have the resources to develop their own AI systems, but they will have resources that allow them to incorporate AI and use it for their benefit. Look for the opportunities created by these technologies.

26

Keep Up The Momentum

With technology constantly evolving at an exponential rate, keeping up with new developments can be challenging. What we know today might change tomorrow, so we need to have a growth mindset and be in constant learning mode.

I've seen a lot of companies make the mistake of implementing a technology system and then thinking that they're sorted for the next ten years. They buy a top-of-the-line computer and six years later they still expect it to be performing well. How can that expensive computer be rubbish now? They don't make these things like they did before!

When our devices were purely mechanical, they worked well for much longer. That's because it wasn't possible to have exponential growth. A cog is a cog; all you can do is add more cogs to make a process a bit faster. With digital, it is different. Software can be improved, and it can adapt to different realities. It can quickly evolve into something different, not just something faster.

The most important thing is not to adopt technology once but to *keep* adopting technology. Don't stop and start; it needs to be a constant evolution. What works well today might not work well tomorrow, and the time between today and tomorrow is getting shorter. When phones used an analogue system, many households had a rotary dial phone. Do you remember the big black box with a circular dial with numbers from 9 to 0? Those phones were introduced in 1904 and they only began to be replaced by push-button phones in the 1970s. Now we change our phones every two years. Whatever phone you own, it won't be available seventy years from now. By replacing our phones every two years, what we are doing is keeping up the momentum. When technology is changing so quickly, if we keep up that momentum then we only need to learn about and adapt to small changes each time. If we let ourselves get behind then when we do eventually have to change it's a massive effort. It's much easier to continuously adapt to small changes than to adapt once to a massive transformation.

This concept applies to our companies too. We put a huge amount of effort and energy into the digital transformation process, so we don't want to waste it. If we don't keep up, all that effort and energy will be lost down the line. We will be left behind, and we will have to start all over again. If we keep feeding our digital transformation process, everything will be much easier because we will just need to make small adjustments.

Digital transformation can't be a project that we start and finish. It needs to be a mindset. When companies develop a digital mindset, digital transformation becomes a constant evolution. It becomes something that we do on a regular basis, not just once. We need to incorporate digital transformation into our companies' DNA. It needs to become natural, part of our companies' culture.

If you have been through a digital transformation in your company, well done – that's a great achievement! You've given your company a strong advantage. Don't let that advantage weaken slowly over time. You have a duty to maintain or even improve that advantage. Keep nurturing your investment, and you will keep collecting the benefits. It's like the laws of motion in physics: it takes more energy to accelerate a stationary object than to maintain the velocity of an object that is already moving.

Keeping up the momentum is crucial for your digital transformation success.

27

My Vision For The Future

Around half of the UK economy is supported by 5.7 million SMEs, while the other half is supported by roughly 8,000 large corporations. These proportions are similar in Europe, in the US and in Asia. However, that imbalance could be corrected if all the world's SMEs were given the right tools – if they invested in technology, if they became innovative, and if they had the right digital strategy.

Why would you want to invert this imbalance? Because SMEs can be better than the large corporations. We as a species function better in small groups than in large ones, because our brains are programmed to operate in close social environments. Dunbar's number suggests that there is a cognitive limit to the number of stable social relationships we can sustain, and that number is 150. We like to belong to a tribe. As social creatures, we are binary: we divide everything into opposites. Us or them. Love or hate. Happy or sad. Work or rest.

Small companies are much more able to create better environments for us humans than large corporations are. Small companies can create purpose and meaning. They can create the feeling of belonging, of being part of 'us'. Imagine if just 10% of the 5.7 million SMEs in the UK became scaleup companies. What impact would that have? How many people would be positively affected?

It's good to work for companies like these because work is part of life. The separation of our work from the rest of our life is a recent phenomenon. For most of human history, work has been 'what we do'. Work is what gave us a sense of purpose. When we were hunting and gathering, there wasn't a separation between work and life. When we started living in settlements, each individual had a profession: the blacksmith, the fishmonger, the baker, the butcher and so on. Then family businesses came along, and different generations worked together to build a better future. It was only with the Industrial Revolution that we started these nine-to-five jobs and entered the rat race. Be unhappy for five days a week at work, because you will be happy for two days at the weekend. Work hard and be miserable for fifty years and if you're lucky, you'll enjoy ten years of happiness when you retire.

Some studies and polls show that 85% of people hate their job.[34] Why do we need to be miserable first to earn the right to be happy later? Why can't we enjoy working?

Here is my vision for the future. SMEs all over the world will be responsible for more than 75% of the world economy, and more than 75% of workers will love their jobs. This vision can be made possible through the adoption of digital technology. That's because digital technology can do, and will do, all the boring jobs we hate and free us up to do the jobs we love. Technology is good at simulating and repeating. On the other hand, we humans excel at creating. Our creativity, imagination, emotions, intuition and uniqueness will be more valuable than our ability to do repetitive tasks.

This is why small companies will be much better prepared for this future. Small companies are nimble, quick, flexible and able to adapt, while large corporations are rigid, slow, inflexible and find it more difficult to adapt (as they manage huge groups of people and resources). Large corporations will be looking for ways to automate, repeat and simulate. Meanwhile, small companies will be looking for ways to be creative, be imaginative and show emotions. These small companies will create the right conditions

---

34 J Clifton (2017) 'The World's Broken Workplace', Gallup, https://news.gallup.com/opinion/chairman/212045/world-broken-workplace.aspx?g_source=position1&g_medium=related&g_campaign=tiles

to promote harmony and give purpose and meaning. The people who will work for these companies will be happy. They will enjoy the present, and their days will be rich and fulfilling. They will have the right to be happy now, rather than having to wait for the chance of happiness in the future.

Acknowledgements

I'd like to thank Daniel Priestley for planting the seed of writing a book in my mind and Lucy McCarraher for making it possible by giving me the framework for writing a book. This book wouldn't have been possible without these two great human beings.

Special thanks go to my staff, Jamie Baker, Adam Braden and Jacob Porter, for allowing me the time and peace of mind to write this book.

Thanks also to James de Vries, my former business partner at Clear IT Solutions, for believing in me and my views on technology and for being crazy enough to start a company with me. His support in the early years of my life in the UK were fundamental for my integration into this great country.

I'd like to acknowledge the United Kingdom for creating the conditions that made it possible for me to transform my dreams into reality. 'Luck is what happens when preparation meets opportunity', as Seneca said.

A special acknowledgement to all the authors of the amazing books I have read over the years. All these people who I don't know personally have had a great impact on my life. They inspired me, they motivated me, they gave me hope and they mentored me. This would be a long list if I mentioned all of them, but without them I would not be the man I am today.

I would also like to acknowledge the KPI community for all the inspirational and motivational stories, examples, successes and failures we have shared.

I'd like to thank everyone who, in any shape or form, has touched my life. It doesn't matter if it was positively or negatively; all of you have helped me to reach where I am today, and I'm grateful for that.

Finally, a special thank you to my lovely wife for her support, inspiration and belief in me and my abilities. She plays an integral and essential part in my life; she complements me and gives me the courage and strength to keep moving forward, never regretting or doubting my actions. Thank you xxx.

Resources

You can download the resources below from www. digital-transformation.website/resources:

- **Activities list:** a template for listing your activities
- **Comparison document:** a template for comparing technologies during your research
- **CLEAR method infographic**
- **Eight Pillars infographic**
- **Hardware replacement plan:** a template for registering your hardware information
- **Procedures document:** a template for documenting your procedures

- **Requirements document:** a template to help you select the right technologies for your company

- **Task list:** a template for listing your tasks and decisions

- **Workflow diagram builder:** explains how to create workflow diagrams

The Author

Nuno Soares began his career in the 1990s as a computer programmer and database developer at a top fifty corporation in Portugal. After a few years as a computer programmer, he was selected to set up and manage the company's internal IT support department. At age twenty-six, he was responsible for a team of four spanning multiple generations. This role exposed Nuno to new technologies that only the big corporations could afford and gave him access to top-level training in business best practice.

In 2001, at the age of twenty-nine, Nuno left his comfortable, well-paid job to start his first company.

His dream was to provide small and medium-sized businesses with the same level of IT support that the big companies could afford. With a growth mindset and with technology becoming more accessible to smaller companies, he built the company to twelve employees and a €1 million turnover. The Portuguese economy suffered during the financial crisis of 2008, and Nuno adapted by downsizing the company, eventually working as a sole trader.

In 2010 Nuno and his family moved to the UK, where he worked for IT companies in Cambridge before setting up a business technology consultancy in 2012. He now helps a broad range of companies across a wide range of industries to transform the way they adopt and integrate technology into their businesses. Nuno's CLEAR (Conscious, Learn, Engineer, Achieve and Resources) method enables companies to identify their current digital position and then plan and execute the right digital transformation strategy for them.

In 2020, as he approaches the age of fifty, Nuno is looking to the next ten years with optimism and excitement. His next challenge is to disrupt the IT market with a new approach to adopting, implementing and embracing digital technologies to make SMEs stronger businesses.

⊕ www.digital-transformation.website